Contemporary House India

Rob Gregory
Photographs by Edmund Sumner

with over 360 illustrations

Contents

Dilemmas of the house

A conversation with B.V. Doshi

Fascinated by architecture's smallest unit of currency – the house – architectural photographer Edmund Sumner and I set out on a number of international ventures to record some of the world's most interesting new homes. Working together, we began in Japan in 2005, bringing the work of Studio Bow-Wow, Sou Fujimoto, Junya Ishigami and others to a wider audience. This was followed by numerous trips to India after Edmund was commissioned to photograph a fashion school in 2008 – the first of over nineteen subsequent visits. Here, longstanding relationships were established with the architects who feature in this book.

In the shadow of such iconic buildings as Le Corbusier's Villa Shodhan (1956) and Villa Sarabhai (1955), both in Ahmedabad, in Gujarat, the dilemma that emerged was how to identify and evaluate the essence of the contemporary Indian home. It is all too easy to get hung up on figure and form, the manipulation of solid and void, the use of concrete, brick and colour, and the placement of furniture. Instead, questions that should be prioritized above and beyond these more measurable attributes include: How does each building respond to the client's attitude to life? How do people want to live? And what does the Indian house tell us about the culture and aspirations of this fascinating nation?

'A house is not just a house, it is a home. It is a community. It is a living entity – and we celebrate this.' B.V. Doshi

For the Pritzker Prize-winning architect Balkrishna Vithaldas Doshi, the house is a template with the potential to address many of architecture's challenges. 'Once we move into a house, generations can grow there, and when generations grow, relationships, attitudes, extensions, modifications and changes happen,' he explains, setting the scene for a conversation that shines a light on the key problem many of the practitioners included here have had to address. How can a new generation of ambitious architects balance their own design aspirations with the needs and wants of their clients to design a house that has the capacity to become a home?

Indian homes that are both successful and authentic, Doshi continues, respond directly to climate and broader issues of sustainability. His definition of sustainability goes beyond connections to the outside world and how to deal with the sun and the rain, and relates to how the house helps sustain family life from one generation to the next. With many families incorporating multiple generations, there is a need for a degree of looseness, informality and flexibility that is less tangible in Western homes. In India, the home hosts celebrations for very large groups of people, so space needs to be accommodating. Multi-generational families have to co-exist, and with this comes the need for a house to evolve with its occupants. 'This affects the nature of expression and experience within the home,' Doshi adds. 'Would the family be a joint family, a larger family, a family of the young and the old? These are the questions that should be asked when designing and building a house.'

'A house should age with its occupants.' B.V. Doshi

A family's experience of living in their house is key to Doshi's reading of a successful home. He cites one of the world's most iconic buildings to help explain how we should prioritize delight over the architect's tendency to over-analyse image, form and composition.

'The first time I thought about Villa Savoye (1931),' he says, 'I was amazed that Le Corbusier, who described the house as a machine for living in, created this particular object in which he doesn't talk about a machine so much as the joy of going around the place. Here, he completely changes, designing a house that is in every way begetting of the kind of things we are talking about; of frozen and rigid things.' So instead of asking questions about style, about why things look the way they do and why compositions took the form they did, Doshi encourages us to ask better questions about the way we live in the places we design.

'Perhaps we shouldn't even use the word "architecture", but instead simply say, "I like to live like this",' he speculates. 'Then there will be a proper dialogue, with proper questions about romance and joy. Are we really raising these questions today when looking at criteria or making judgements?'

Returning to Villa Savoye, Doshi continues to challenge the way we prioritize architectural order, describing how the house is conventionally read as an essay in composition. Instead, he says, we should focus on how Le Corbusier intended the spaces to be experienced, rather than how they can be seen. 'It is a very unusual demonstration of an object in which you can rejoice in experiences and, if you like, still live in and enjoy,' he explains. 'At a high level is the spatial experience, but at the highest level it is seen as an object. We must reverse this order. Le Corbusier said, "I am talking about architecture." But what is architecture? It is an experience, a spatial experience – I would like to use that experience as place in which you can also live.'

So while the composition of the Villa Savoye includes all of the things that the resident may need – a courtyard, a little garden, a nice view, terraces, a solarium, some rooms – and is a hugely significant piece of design, it first and foremost answers all of the questions that we really need to ask. 'What Le Corbusier is saying is that anybody who comes here will enjoy the experience,' Doshi continues. 'The solarium, everyone will enjoy. The terrace, everyone will enjoy. And everyone can look out the window and enjoy the landscape.'

'But when have you ever seen a house with a ramp? It is the journey that Le Corbusier stretches, showing that he really understood experience and how to create a journey with all the experiences around it. This is his real contribution.' B.V. Doshi

Doshi also looks to his other former mentor and boss, Louis Kahn, to illustrate how we should reverse the order in which we judge the buildings around us, citing Kahn's subtle spatial genius. Although Kahn did not design any of India's key Modernist homes, Doshi nonetheless calls on him to illustrate his commentary on the sort of improvisation exhibited in Le Corbusier's ramp in his longstanding text, *The Acrobat and the Yogi* (1993). 'Improvisation is an attitude,' Doshi begins, before describing the sort of urban improvisation that comes from the looser kinds of buildings and streets typical of his home city, Ahmedabad.

This is evident in the dormitories of Kahn's Indian Institute of Management, which he worked on from 1962 until his death in 1974, where there are enclaves and niches in the wall and the spaces become very narrow. 'He did all of this without saying why,' Doshi continues. 'But if you go and walk there, you will know that he was responding to people's longing for shade, for meandering movements, for leisurely ways of working. And then you go to the classroom, with large heights, and you know this is something else that is completely formal.'

'Louis Kahn manipulated heights and volumes, so you could feel part of a hot climate, with places where people could be still, or could walk slowly. He played it very well.' B.V. Doshi

In this, Doshi is extending his challenge for today's architects to reverse the order of their intentions, to focus on spatial experience over formal composition to respond to people's needs and have something genuinely relevant and meaningful to say about architecture and its response to people's day-to-day life. Returning to the scale of the home, he goes on to describe how there is little distinction between designing a home for 500 people, a single dwelling or a building of a completely different type, as is it always about creating space for the occupants to have their experience of life enhanced.

'Scale is only an extension,' he says, as he recalls the approach taken when designing a housing project in 1973 for the Life Insurance Corporation, also in Ahmedabad, where he reversed the typical order of multi-residential housing by placing the largest homes on the ground level, and the smallest on the top floor. This was done to avoid the typical format of separate ghettos and 'to efface the distinction between different income groups in society'. Instead, he says, over time, 'everyone was accommodated and negotiated their place. And this is really the purpose in creating a social structure. It was to empower people – of different castes, religions, beliefs, or from different regions – and today they are all living together and feeling like a community. What architecture tends to do is separate the people out. So we were going against the grain.'

Doshi's focus on human experience over architectural posturing extends further to show how architecture needs to evolve and respond to human and broader forms of nature. An understanding of nature's order is essential, he says, to ensure the buildings and places we build enhance people's ability to experience life.

'This is, of course, how nature has evolved,' he adds, recalling how impressed he was with the animals he saw at the zoo. 'It impressed me immensely, because I saw crocodiles, camels, hippos and birds. I could never understand how nature creates such completely different characters that are so integrally aligned with their habitat. Absolute sustenance. They know how to be in the weather, how to get food, how to defend themselves and their young – there is not one question that has been not answered.' So while modern houses may appear ubiquitous, if we look deeper into the nature of place and the nature of people, much more can be revealed about how these buildings function as homes.

'Architecture is incidental. But we are hooked on that word, and that is the problem. We don't talk about life, we don't talk about living. I think this is where the issue lies.' B.V. Doshi

And so we conclude our conversation with me beginning to question the very purpose of this book – the purpose of architectural theory, of analysis of plans, sections and elevations, and the description of different approaches to craft and construction. But once again, the ninety-two-year-old Doshi reveals himself to be nimbler and more astute, by reversing the order when I ask if analysis of craft, form and detail have stolen the show for too long.

'No, no,' he asserts, reassuringly. 'Just don't give them a name. Don't separate them. While these terms have existed for a long time, people are alienated by saying "this is craft", "this is technology", and so on. Analysis has freaked our brain and our attitude to life. If you just use the word "dwelling" for everything, and print it like that, nobody will question what it is.'

'Critics come along and connect you to history, and tell you why it is right or wrong, without really knowing what it means. This is no way to learn from something, or to expand our horizons.' B.V. Doshi

So when looking at this small survey of homes, we try to do so with new eyes, as we attempt to understand the essence of the contemporary Indian house. We ask, why is there an overhang here, or a courtyard there? Why has this house got more windows, and this one fewer? We want you to step inside the minds of the architect and, more importantly, the client, in order to better understand the design decisions. By doing so, we hope the nature of each home will reveal itself in a unique way, by focusing on the particular aspirations and experiences of life that make these groups of houses unique, identifying the essence of the contemporary Indian house.

Dilemmas of the architect

Reflections of today's practitioners

The day after my interview with B. V. Doshi, I invited the architects featured in this book to a specially convened symposium at the school of architecture at CEPT University, in Ahmedabad, to discuss their work. The purpose of the event was to learn more about each project and to identify what continuities and points of difference exist between generations. Interestingly, despite my assumption that a divide would soon open up, it doesn't take long for Le Corbusier and the impact of Modernism to emerge as a key topic of conversation.

'If there had been no communication, if no one had seen Le Corbusier, what would Indian architecture be today?' Samira Rathod

Mumbai-based architect Samira Rathod (Broacha House, p. 154; Shadow House, p. 182) makes the first reference to Corbusier. Despite her own pursuit of a form of architectural practice that is devoid of 'isms', and an acknowledgment that Modernism was intended to liberate us from bygone modes of architecture, she is clear that Le Corbusier and Louis Kahn remain as enduring legacies of the last century, with shadows that still loom large.

With work that covers all scales, from the city to the single private home, the re-contextualized Modernism of Corbusier and Kahn brought a radical alternative to other imported influences, such as that of Sir Edwin Lutyens, so heavily imposed on New Delhi. Gone was any play on architecture's established classical language or use of decorative ornamentation, and in its place were bold new forms of architecture that responded to the people and places they served. Responsive to climate and to the rituals of public and domestic life, the parliaments, assemblies, universities and residences of Corbusier and Kahn demonstrated Modernism's ability, in the right hands, to truly respond to a range of human needs that transcend cultures and contexts.

In India, their influence lived on through a number of key practitioners, including Charles Correa, Raj Rewal and Doshi, who inspired the generation of design leaders that followed. Today, however, the profession is less tightly defined, intellectually re-programmed by those who left India to study in Europe and America, and delivered by an increasingly large number of new recruits trained in one of the hundreds of schools of architecture that now exist. So while Indian architects are generating entirely new, twenty-first-century culture, the identity of the country's architecture has become less easy to define.

Introduction

Back at the symposium, Pinkish Shah of S&PS Architects (Collage House, p. 56) notes that today's architects face a different set of struggles than Doshi and his generation, and try actively to resist universal internationalism by working within a series of distinct regional identities. Arjun Malik of Malik Architecture (House at Alibag, p. 192; Lagoon Residence, p. 202; House of Three Streams, p. 212) describes the 'reactionary' approach he pursued on returning from Columbia University in New York as a response to 'the tyranny of the concrete frame, which had absolved architecture from asking the most fundamental questions relating to place, time and human interaction'.

But while the challenges that face them may be different, what unites today's practitioners with the previous generation is the call to re-order our appraisal of Modernism, as all of the contributors, without exception, agreed with the need to prioritize our experience of architecture above and beyond any intellectual reading of its formal and compositional pursuits. As Samira Rathod notes: 'While Modernism liberates you from many -isms, it creates its own. So we always take our cues from conversations with our clients, as the context of the project is much larger than its site. We always begin with basic questions. What do you do when you get up? What kind of rooms do you like? What spaces do you enjoy? Through this, a new set of architectural challenges emerge.'

The caution about the scope of this survey of new buildings is, of course, unavoidable, as this is a book about luxury homes. What it brought to the conversation, however, were richer, broader narratives about the state of modern architecture in India today and how to break down stereotypical views about architectural practice; the legacy and future of India's craft-based construction industry; the challenges of working for the super-rich; and the new tyranny of Pinterest and the dilution of authentic approaches to interior design.

Stereotypes

'Playful' is one of the words that sparks a response from this generation of architects, who recognize with regret that it is still the case that primary architectural discourse comes from the West, imposing views that take little input from those who are actually shaping the subject. Having trained in New York, Arjun Malik seems best placed to raise this issue, and maintains that, in his view, Western critics and academics are driving the debate.

'The West still drives design direction, and when looking to South East Asia and India, this sometimes brings a stereotypical patronizing attitude that Indian architecture favours beauty, ornamentation and celebration.' Arjun Malik

'If you're trying to be seen as serious within the fraternity,' he says, with revealing frustration, 'these terms seem to be marginalized, as if it's not done to keep talking about composition or ornament and expression.'

With a challenge to his peers, noting how Japan and China are succeeding in getting emerging design and architectural philosophies out there, Malik concludes: 'We simply haven't been able to push into the mainstream and build an overall ethos, other than in individual silos. So now we need to gather momentum collectively.'

But what might a new Indian architectural ethos look like?

Human resources

One of India's largest natural resources is its labour force, which is why craft is such a sustainable and economical solution. Unlike so much of the rest of the world, where craft is extremely expensive, in India craft skills have been passed down from generation to generation, resulting in a cumulative intelligence developed over a long period of time. But how long will this continue? Delhi-based Verendra Wakhloo of Matra Architects (Jenga House, p. 30; Kaleka Residence & Studios, p. 38; Wood House, p. 99) is keen to take an optimistic view, noting that while Europe experienced a 300-year rift between craft and industrialization, 'India has only had fifty years. Before the rift becomes any bigger, we should look at our responsibilities as architects and create a manifesto that considers what is intrinsic to the dynamics of this culture of the handmade.'

While acknowledging the richness of Indian craft and the quality of handmade buildings, Arjun Malik raises a note of caution: 'We keep talking about craft being available to us at a low cost, but there is a danger that we fetishize and romanticize it. The fact is that with the overbearing thorns of an unresolved imperialistic outlook, the moment we say we want to give craft some form of dignity, and enable people to make a livelihood from it, it will inevitably start to become really expensive.'

Going further, he concludes by saying, 'there is a slightly hypocritical association with craft-based industry, and it needs to be looked into as a socio-cultural phenomenon. Because this is what people are looking for from India, and we pander to them as architects. We can see it through international publications and exhibitions. There are a lot of terms that are being used flippantly to look for answers from India.'

'Craftwork involves working with your hands. It means working in the sun. But it is not afforded great dignity. As such, there is a danger that the next generation won't want to touch it.' Arjun Malik

But does the rising cost of craft matter, when for centuries some of our most celebrated examples of architecture would not have existed were it not for the patronage of the super-rich? Clearly it does, as architects working today seem frustrated by the lack of opportunities to engage in the sort of socially based projects that challenged Doshi and his generation, and feel forced instead to work, somewhat reluctantly, for the so-called 'burgeoning middle classes' and rising elite. And with this, thanks to a neat summary by Verendra Wakhloo, the conversation liberates itself from the issue of identity, and comes swiftly back down to earth to acknowledge the unavoidable fact that these luxury homes are a playoff between the personal agendas of the architects and their wealthy clients. In facing this challenge, this generation of architects are finding new ways of working in which they can maintain their integrity as designers.

Client dynamics

'The problem is that when you get into projects of a certain budget, when someone is able to afford a 25,000 sq ft (over 2,300 m²) home, that client is obviously very wealthy,' admits one of the architects in the room. So how do architects balance the demands of wealthy clients with their own ambitions to demonstrate the social purposes of their art?

When it comes to working with wealthy clients, strong tensions quickly emerge, with Samira Rathod describing interior design as 'open season' between architect and client. 'There is a chasm between our clients and us, and we have to constantly demonstrate and resist and fight,' she explains. 'I usually do this by saying, "If you don't like it, I will pay for it," and that seems to work, by making it clear that we are on their side.' This, in part, stems from a knowledge gap, with few clients paying particular interest to the bones of the buildings.

Another voice echoes: 'The external art of architecture, the formation of space and volume and the understanding of climate is beyond the realm of understanding for most clients. Once the shell is built, they are finally able to understand and visualize, and start asking for this material and that finish. This is when they turn to their Pinterest, or boutique hotels for inspiration. One might assume that someone that wealthy and well travelled would have an understanding of architecture and space, but unlike other art forms, such as music and cinema, architecture is much less discussed in contemporary society – and that hurts. They literally don't get it.'

Gurjit Singh Matharoo of Matharoo Associates (House of Balls, p. 226; Fissured Living, p. 231; Stripped Mobius, p. 244; Moving Landscapes, p. 256) offers a different opinion, drawing on his experience of designing homes for India's super-rich, with a catalogue of amusing but insightful observations into their demands. These include requests for large glazed windows, despite the region's searing heat, elaborate technical devices to impress guests, and the sensitivities associated with inevitable tensions of large, multi-generational families. Despite this, he concludes, 'most of our good ideas come from the client'.

'Each client is different, so you latch on to the peculiarities and bring it into your design. On the one hand, there is a big challenge. But on the other, you have to use the client's force to get something you like.' Gurjit Singh Matharoo

Pinkish Shah concurs by focusing on the need for strong architectural ideas, noting that client relationships can be very vulnerable. 'The seed of the idea has to be very strong, so the quality of the project is robust,' he explains, before Samira Rathod concludes the discussion by returning the responsibility firmly to the designer, reminding the students in the audience that, ultimately, it is the architect's job to have those negotiations with the client, and to steer them in a direction that they will never have seen or thought of.

'You will have scenarios where clients come with a brief that is unsustainable, as they can afford anything as individuals,' she cautions. 'But, as a nation, we cannot afford to do certain things, so we need to drive to a smaller footprint, or mode of use. By doing so, the notion of luxury can be re-presented to the client, and you will gain huge credibility and trust. We as architects must take on this element of expertise.'

Closing thoughts

What conclusions can be drawn? Robert Verrijt, founder of Architecture Brio (Tala Treehouse Villa, p. 144; House on a Stream, p. 172), brings a degree of critical distance to the conversation. Having been born and trained in the Netherlands, before spending the majority of his professional life practising in India, he believes that the identity crisis and search for narrative are red herrings, chiming with Doshi's earlier comments about the over-intellectualization of domestic architectural mores. 'I even question the need to create a common narrative,' he adds. 'In the Netherlands, you are not asked if your work has a Dutch identity or a European one. You do not question the historical reality of Modernism (or let us say classicism). I think we should be open to more diversity and embrace new possibilities. The world is becoming less homogenous.'

And the reality in India is even more profound, with one contributor describing it as 100 countries in one.

'There are endless theories and ideologies that have come before, it is not necessary to say "this is who I am". There is an enormous danger that in promoting a single identity, you leave out a lot of other stories and people.' Robert Verrijt

Verendra Wakhloo concludes the conversation by returning to Le Corbusier: 'We know that Corbusier's shadow is big, but he is still an inspiration. He was always looking into the future. We should do the same, projecting what India will look like in fifty years. We should be developing an agenda and reducing India's carbon footprint. Even though we may not like someone's opulent brief, we remain compelled to fulfil it. We beautify it, but our desire is not to please a client, that is banal. We like to take a more socially responsible approach. We are very restrained in our expression. There seems to be a collective consciousness that is telling us we are not living in a superfluous society, that we have to be super-conscious in our work. We can show how it can be done better. Quick, cheap and beautiful. I think there is a voice here. It is the DNA of our past.'

Clearly, the voice of Le Corbusier still resonates today.

One

Urban Living

Urban Living:
Challenging typologies

Radhika Villa
Ahmedabad, Gujarat
Vastushilpa Consultants

Indian cities, like most in the world, are experiencing great change. While some critics focus on the increased densification and height that mass housing can bring, it is also interesting to consider how the single, one-off house is contributing to changes in urban living. Global typologies abound: the terrace, or row house; the townhouse; the semi-detached or detached house. House typologies such as the bungalow are important reference points for large projects. Sharing responsibility for the future of Doshi's studio Vastushilpa Consultants, his son-in-law Rajeev Kathpalia brings continuity to its portfolio of work by extending the firm's widely recognized contribution to social and affordable housing into larger development types, including a number of new university campuses. As for many architects, for Kathpalia the design of the single dwelling unlocked ideas for larger projects and ambitions.

When it was built in 2009, Radhika Villa was the latest addition to a small private street in a suburb of western Ahmedabad. Known as a housing society development, such streets or areas are typically brought to market by developers who parcel up plots for families to take on individually, and vary from gated enclaves to more permeable communities – the latter being the type chosen by Kathpalia for his own home. The plot resembles a European cul-de-sac, complete with a communal garden and clubhouse at the end of the street, and the architectural challenge was to maximize the space between the houses, so that Kathpalia and his family could enjoy both their own and their neighbour's garden, without diminishing any sense of privacy. He did this by positioning windows and rooflights, setting up diagonal views across the house to take in specific vistas, trees and clear sky.

The pursuit of privacy in the city does not demand isolation, so the house is distinguished by a series of spaces that are full of light and air. It also adapts urban devices that encourage interaction and brings them into the heart of the home, including a large

'The house informs the potential of things. In going back and forth between the scales of a single house, a university campus and collective housing, you are able to begin talking about cities and systems. The idea of space, your journey through it and your experience of it are still important, regardless of scale.'

Rajeev Kathpalia

1

1 The principal façade provides different
degrees of shelter and privacy.

Radhika Villa

2

3

Urban Living

2 The house sits in a quiet
residential street adjacent to
mid-rise accommodation.
3 From street level, the water tower
is seen to rise up from barely visible
ceramic roof surfaces.
4, 5 With relatively small gardens
in this suburban setting, the roof
terrace provides additional space.

5

4

hall, inspired by a traditional Indian *otla*, a series of steps built
outside townhouses, where people would sit out and engage with
passers-by. Although there are few passers-by in the neighbourhood, Kathpalia used this device to form a focus of family life.
So while the rooms that surround the hall are characterized in
terms of how they relate to the outside world and the immediate
landscape, they all share a direct link to the double-height hall that
cranks on plan to add a further sense of dynamism.

Parents and children can either retreat to their own private rooms,
enjoying fine views through the beautifully detailed teak windows and shutters, or
venture outside and find their own place within this mini-piazza, which achieves its
own sense of urbanity through the use of fine stone (in this case, Jaisalmer stone,
laid as found in large, irregular pieces). With a series of high-level internal balconies
and windows, this sophisticated piece of architecture heightens the ambiguous
nature of this pivotal internal/external space.

As Kathpalia notes, the social aspects of urban homes have never been so important, as the domestic public realm is increasingly under threat by the type of houses
being brought to the market. 'There was a time when you would only need to build
one house in your lifetime,' he says. 'Now the dynamics of the market and access
to finance mean that most people will have many houses. Young homeowners are
more prevalent, and the commodification of the home is part of broader change.'

The houses featured in this chapter show alternatives to this, with a new generation
of multi-generation, multi-use, long-life urban homes.

6

7

6 Rooflights frame and capture
views of the immediate landscape.
7 Exposed concrete provides a
consistent background for built-in
furniture and fine joinery windows.

Urban Living

Jenga House
New Delhi, Delhi
Matra Architects

'In this neighbourhood, the porosity of space and form encourages connection to the neighbourhood and the city, and develops the possibility of future living.'

Verendra Wakhloo

Likened by some to the game of Jenga, this house by Matra Architects plays on a balance between solid and void. For architect Verendra Wakhloo, the formal playfulness is an antidote to the reduction of open space in our cities – a condition he attributes to modern housing with unusable space between neighbouring homes, typically adorned with balconies for air-conditioning, plants, rear elevations littered with pipes and services, and a decorative mask-like façade that tries but fails to bring identity to the street.

By contrast, Jenga House is open on all sides and features two primary L-shaped units that stack and interlock to create a series of interstitial courtyards and terraces. Hovering above the ground and overlapping like yin and yang, two full-length floors of accommodation on levels one and four contain the family's living spaces, service areas and guest accommodation. These are counterbalanced by smaller floor plates on levels two and three, which retreat from each other to provide more private space for each family's principal sleeping accommodation.

Additional degrees of porosity are achieved through the carving out of internal courtyards, which relate more directly to specific internal rooms, and reductions in width that open up long views from the back of the site through to the street. Both of these moves also serve to reduce the apparent mass and potential monotony of the wood-shuttered cast concrete that extends across the site.

To provide a backdrop for the client's requested European-inspired interiors, Wakhloo introduced very few additional materials, with exposed aggregate, metal reveals and cable-tensioned guarding articulating the otherwise simple rectangular apertures. The exception to this muted material palette is a number of carefully detailed steel staircases – the distinctively steep and narrow 'samba' stairs, with alternating steel treads punched and bent from a single sheet of mild steel, before being clad in brass by hand, and a number of winding stairs featuring a variety of painted steel and glazed stair treads. Two of these are encased in concrete cores, which form the principal mode of support and help articulate each of the two units, with cantilevers of up to 4.5 to 6 m (15 to 20 ft).

'For us the brief of the client is secondary, because all clients want the same thing; *pooja* rooms to the north, south-facing master bedrooms, and so on,' Wakhloo explains. 'All briefs are similar – the areas vary, the relationships vary, but they are only a minor challenge for any architect. For us, the city is the challenge.'

1 (previous page) From the street, the house provides extended views through the margins of the site.
2 The building comprises two L-shaped blocks of accommodation, each with double storeys that interlock by stepping up or down.

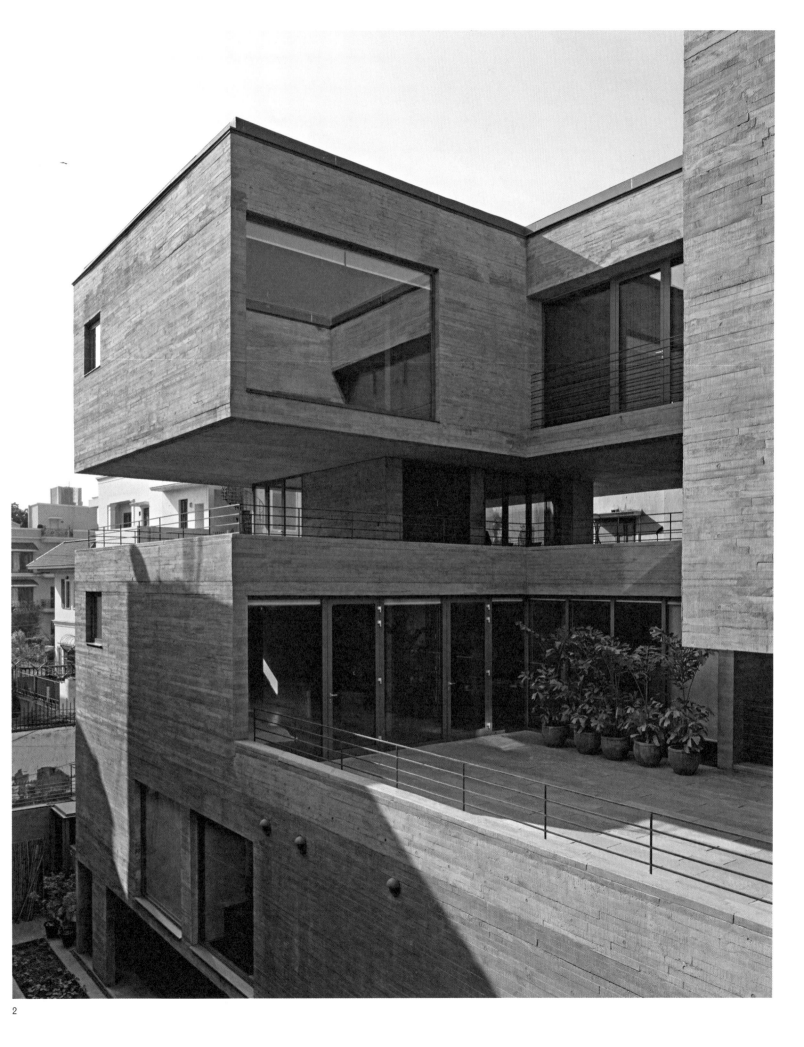

2

Jenga House

3

Urban Living

4

3 The composition provides
generous external spaces that
benefit from varying degrees
of shelter and privacy.
4 Smaller external spaces are
presented as simple cut-outs
in the concrete walls.

Jenga House

5

6

7

8

9

10

5–8 Against a neutral backdrop of exposed concrete walls, internal spaces are articulated by stairs, each with their own character.

9 Above the 'stilt floor', raised ground-floor spaces are arranged around the main arrivals stair.
10 A brass-clad 'samba' stair is suspended at the centre of the ground-floor living rooms.

Jenga House

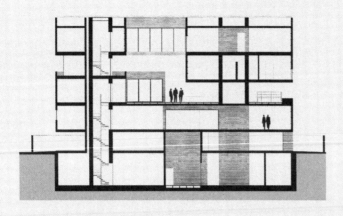

11

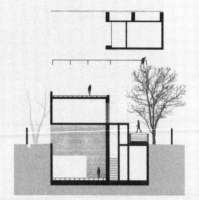

12

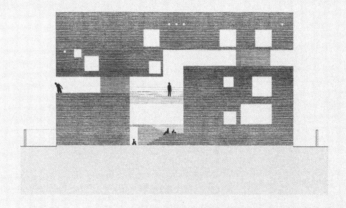

13

14

11, 12 Sections
13 Entrance / north elevation
14 Terrace / south elevation

Urban Living

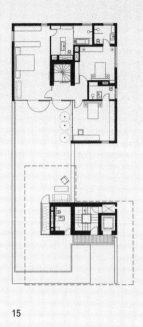

15

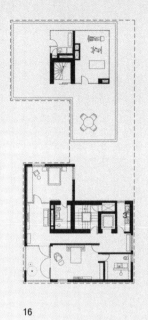

16

17

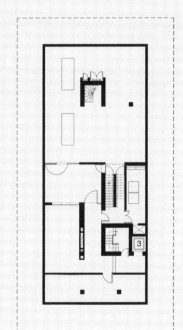

18

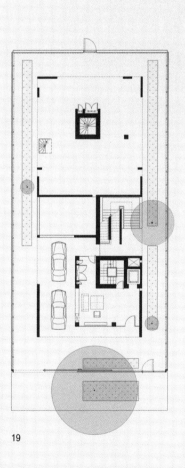

19

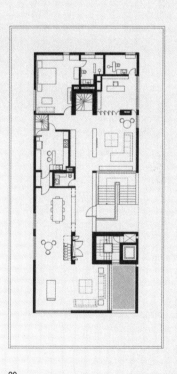

20

15 First-floor plan
16 Second-floor plan
17 Third-floor plan
18 Basement plan
19 Stilt-floor plan
20 Ground-floor plan

Jenga House

Kaleka Residence & Studios
Greater Noida, Uttar Pradesh
Matra Architects

'Building for the artists was an act of rebellion. Manifesting the studio for the vulnerable artists protected against the invasion of different views and of strangers looking in. It became very fortified building.'

Verendra Wakhloo

This pair of robust rough concrete structures by Matra Architects occupy a prominent position in a new suburban neighbourhood developed for a community of artists, 40 km (25 miles) southeast of Delhi. Their distinctive stepped silhouettes combine to form a gateway at the intersection of three octagonal clusters of accommodation and provide spaces for working and living across both plots.

It was always understood that the brief would be an act of rebellion against the prescriptive development codes (sanctioned by the clients, who requested two identical buildings without windows). Ignoring the strict rules dictating what the façades should look like and what materials should be used means that these buildings are yet to be signed off and may never be fully approved. Despite this, the clients are happy to live in them and to enjoy the immersive environment held within.

Contrary to their bullish rebellion, the artistic vulnerability of the clients is seen in their desire to have spaces that are fortified, avoiding the scrutiny of others while they work. They did, however, want plenty of natural light, so the design includes a series of steps in section that allows light to fall into the space with suitable degrees of drama and dynamism. The houses also exploit the expression of handmade sculptures, cast in extremely rough concrete, whose imperfections are exaggerated as light falls from above. This, of course, provides a canvas and backdrop for the clients' work, which employs coloured canvases and video installations. It will also be allowed to get dirty over time.

In contrast to these random and uneven surfaces, the next most prominent elements are the angular steel stair guards, which twist, turn, bend and buckle their way through the three principal floors of accommodation, which rise up from the sunken courtyard and basement studio and through the double-height living room and mezzanine. Above this, accessed by a winding steel spiral stair is a tightly planned floor that takes on a penthouse format with bedroom, kitchenette, dining and bathing areas, and provides a place where husband and wife can meet.

While a proposal to link each of the plots at top-floor level with a retractable bridge is yet to be agreed or implemented, the architect has confirmed that the houses have proven to be extremely popular among other artists in the community. Standing strong against the rules of engagement with the site's development code, they have also become emblematic of an artist's role in society of questioning conventions, with many of the neighbours voicing regret about not breaking the rules themselves.

1 These two studios provide living and working accommodation for a pair of artists, southeast of Delhi.

Kaleka Residence & Studios

2

2 Impenetrable from the outside,
from the street little is given away
about what goes on inside.
3 On walking around the corner, the
sculptural and symmetrical forms of
the studios begin to reveal slithers
of glazing and signs of life within.

Urban Living

4

5

6

4–6 Stairs articulate each of the
internal spaces, with diagonal
flights rising three storeys,
culminating in a tight spiral stair
that gives access to the living
accommodation and winter
garden on the top floor.
7 A mezzanine within the main
volume features a large artist's
bench along its balcony edge.
8 Living spaces at the top of
each studio are more intimately
scaled, with less drama than the
voluminous studios below.

Urban Living

7

8

Kaleka Residence & Studios

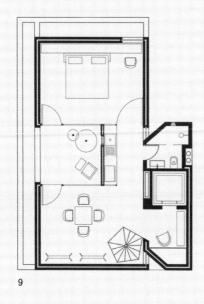

9

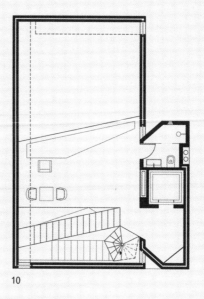

10

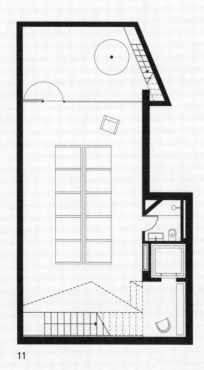

11

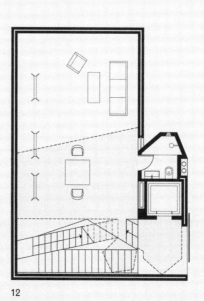

12

9 First-floor plan
10 Mezzanine plan
11 Basement plan
12 Ground-floor plan

Urban Living

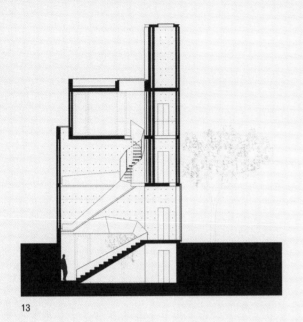

13

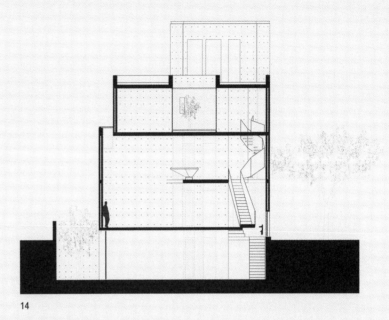

14

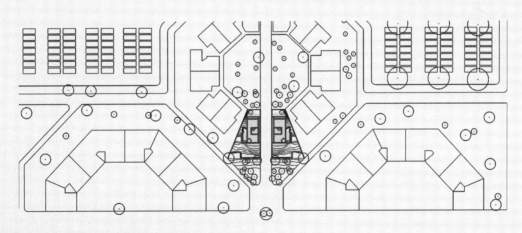

15

13, 14 Sections
15 Site plan

Kaleka Residence & Studios

Brick House
New Delhi, Delhi
Romi Khosla Design Studios

The urban conditions that this house, designed by Romi Khosla Design Studios, negotiates include the sharply tapering geometry of the plot and a number of pre-existing mature trees, which sit just beyond the site boundary. Designed for a family of four, and to accommodate regular visits from grandparents, the living space is broken down into three distinct blocks, which provide communal, private and service spaces in a prominent composition open to the neighbourhood on three sides.

To the rear, where the site is at its broadest, the 22 m (72 ft)-wide boundary is pinned down by a slender, tower-like form that contains all of the house's service and staff accommodation. Instead of being relegated to a basement or tucked away in hidden corners of the site, the tower gives a certain prominence and pride to what are often neglected spaces. It also sets up the formal and material language for the rest of the property, which comprises two blocks that are more squat in form, and broaden, step down, change material and open up to fine views into the neighbouring trees in a controlled, four-stage transition.

The central block mimics the tower's brick-and-steel elevations and contains the main arrival, circulation and cellular spaces. On ground level and on axis with the entrance is the *pooja* room (an area for prayer), while to the left is the main stair, leading to four upper levels that contain the kitchen and dining space on the upper ground floor, and a range of bedrooms and studies on the first, second and third floors.

Each of these more private levels leads to one of three spacious communal areas, with the entrance and upper-ground floors leading through to a double-height space articulated by balcony and stair, which hunkers down to address a tranquil sunken garden. Above, the first and second floors have access to an almost identical space, distinguished by a balcony that cuts across at an angle, and by elevated views directly into the tree canopy. Above this double stack of duplexes, the third floor leads onto an expansive roof terrace.

Lead architect Martand Khosla notes that the influence of Le Corbusier is expressed in this house through the use of colour, mainly applied to connecting vertical surfaces, from the green that articulates the principal stair to the flash of yellow glimpsed through the tower's three-storey slot window.

1 This new family home is distinguished by a slender brick tower, standing guard next to the main point of entry.

1

Brick House

Urban Living

3

2 Away from the entrance, two double-height living rooms are stacked one above the other to form a four-storey louvred façade.
3 The main accommodation block is articulated in steel and brick, distinct from the narrower wing of living rooms to the left.

Brick House

4

Urban Living

5

4, 5 Throughout the day, louvres, windows and lighting bring dynamism to this home's strong composition.

Brick House

6

7

Urban Living

8

6 On entry, the first splash of colour
is seen, articulating the main stair.
7 Each of the living rooms is
distinct, here with a dramatic angle
to the mezzanine edge.
8 The upper-most double-height
living room gains privacy from the
adjacent tree canopies.

Brick House

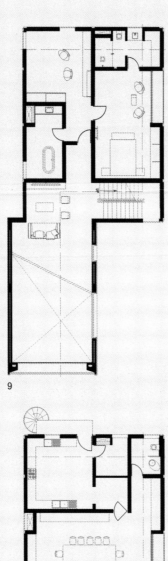

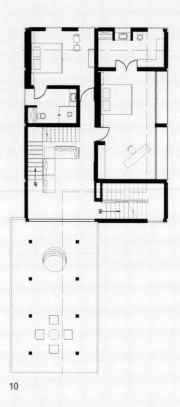

9

10

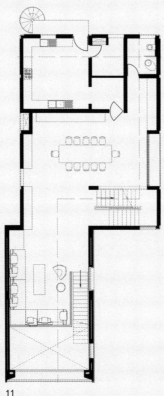

11

12

9 Third-floor plan
10 Second-floor plan
11 Ground-floor plan
12 First-floor plan

Urban Living

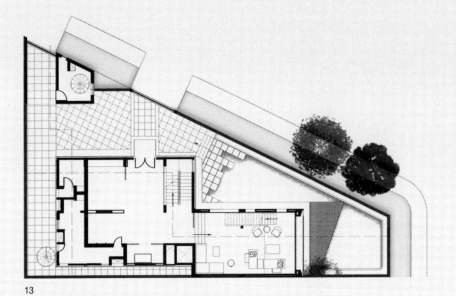

13

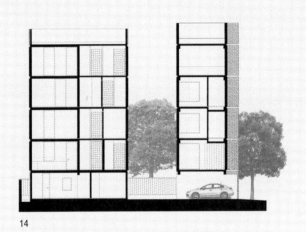

14

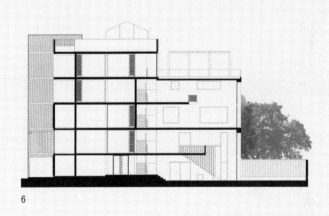

6

16

17

13 Site plan
14, 15 Sections
16, 17 Elevations

Collage House
Navi Mumbai, Maharashtra
S&PS Architects

'Sustainability has begun to create a box-ticking culture. We felt this was problematic – despite good intentions, it has led to soulless spaces that were lacking quality.'

Pinkish Shah

Collage House by S&PS Architects combines a number of urban constraints with an ambitious and creative approach to sustainability and upcycling. As part of a new residential suburb designed by renowned Indian architect Charles Correa and his team, the plot is situated across the harbour in Mumbai and takes on a number of planning setbacks and security measures, which helped to shape the structure's principal concrete form. Set within this main frame are myriad materials and interlocking spaces that combine to create a unique full-time family home for four generations.

Despite its elevated position, neighbouring properties limit distant views, so spaces were planned around a centralized inner courtyard, providing a focus for family life and a place where everyone can come together. Cubic in proportion, this double-height space allows the house to harness Mumbai's breezes, providing cross-ventilation to all of the habitable spaces. It also sits alongside the required planning setback, which has been efficiently colonized to contain a pool at courtyard level and a formal stepped entrance from the forecourt. Natural ventilation and exposed thermal mass are not the only environmental measures this house employs, as a shared interest in waste soon became a focus for the creative collaboration between architect and client.

As the world's fifth-largest generator of waste, it is incumbent upon all of Mumbai's communities to play their part in reducing waste and promoting recycling. Residents of informal communities are leading the way, demonstrating enterprising approaches. Against this backdrop, Collage House brings a resourcefulness to communities that might otherwise expect everything to be built from new, along with a sense of authenticity and character to this new suburb.

With parallel references that draw upon the art of Joseph Cornell, Richard Hamilton and Louise Nevelson, client and architect began sourcing materials and building components that included metal sheeting and pipes and large quantities of stone from on-site enabling works and excavation. The most prominent of these is the collection of historic doors and windows, which were sourced by the client, a businessman who spent his Sundays scouting out local reclamation yards. Once measured, photographed and documented, elements like these were integrated into the architect's palette of materials and detailed accordingly, resulting – in the case of the principal façade – in a suspended curtain wall with a collage of antique timber and contemporary polycarbonate sheeting.

Other quirky highlights include the decorative use of industrial wire mesh to create a *jali* screen for the lift and a laminated glass wall for the *pooja* room. The home's smallest space – the powder room – is clad on all walls and the ceiling in antique mirrored tiles, producing apparently infinite kaleidoscopic reflections. The architect also managed to skilfully integrate the 100-year-old decorative columns that support the modern metal penthouse canopy – the icing on the client's cake.

1 Collage by name, collage by nature: this house is characterized by the integration of antique doors and windows, set within an otherwise unadorned polycarbonate-and-concrete façade.

1

Collage House

2

2 The house is arranged around
a double-height courtyard, which
extends into a mandatory open setback.
3 Modern cladding and screens and
antique doors and windows combine
to create a variety of spatial conditions.

Urban Living

3

Collage House

4

5

4, 5   Articulated by its collage
wall, the main living room is further
distinguished by its cast-concrete
coffered ceiling.

6

7

6, 7 The house is punctuated by other quirky optical delights, seen here in the powder room and the prayer room.

Collage House

9

8, 9 The principal stair and *jali* screen
rise through all four floors, starting in
the cosy entrance hall above.

Collage House

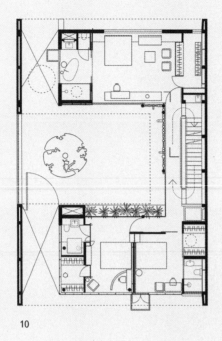

10

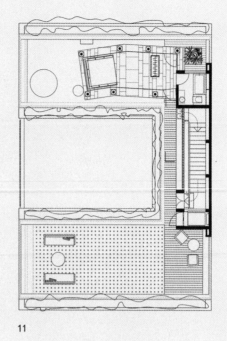

11

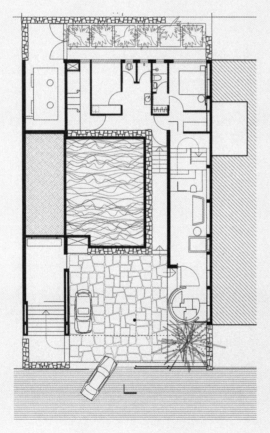

12

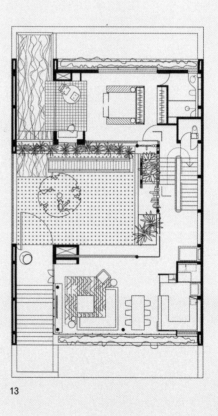

13

10–13 Floor plans

Urban Living

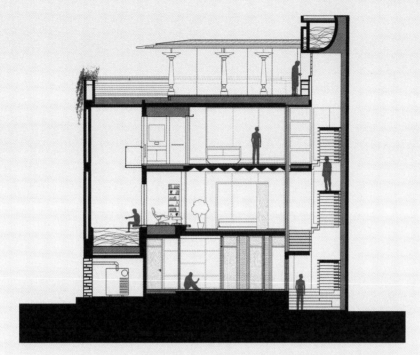

14

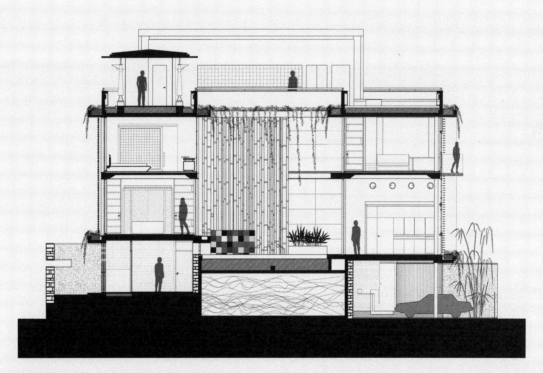

15

14, 15 Sections

Collage House

Lattice House
Jammu City, Jammu
Sameep Padora & Associates

'With the immediate landscape compromised by the lack of government intervention, the house becomes a function for a need of structured form. The lack of a distinct contextual urban fabric (apart from the pylons) also projects its role as a distinct urban marker visible from a distance, its material singularity seen in sharp contrast.'

Sameep Padora

Lattice House, when read as an essay in duality, becomes emblematic of the stark contrasts that co-exist within India's constantly developing urban context. Located in a new suburb on the outskirts of Jammu City in northwestern India, and described by its architect as an 'urban marker', this provocative structure is much more than a private home, giving form to the relatively unregulated process of rapid, chaotic change that many urban communities are having to face.

Displaying little in the way of traditional domesticity and sharing more in common with the neighbouring pylons, this imposing structure could at first glance be mistaken for a piece of much-needed new infrastructure – a substation or pumping station, perhaps, screened by what appear to be rusty metal gratings. On closer inspection, however, the 'metal' is revealed as the finely detailed timber panels of a bold and highly conspicuous new private home.

Rising above neighbouring properties, yet providing only two storeys above ground, the secretive screened façades give the impression of a much larger multi-storey property, as the bands of timber slats wrap round and jetty out in three stages. While the uppermost layer serves mainly as a parapet to the large flat roof, the lower pair enclose one of two residential suites, screening windows and external courtyards and providing shade and shelter from the region's extremely hot and dry climate.

At ground level and largely hidden from sight by a white masonry boundary wall, the second, more private family home benefits from the shade of the jettied overhangs and direct access to a series of private subdivided courtyards, terraces and garden rooms. With domestic life centred around entertaining and hospitality, the kitchen is placed at the centre of the plan, flanked by living and dining spaces on one side, and a private lawn on the other. Bedrooms and other private spaces are located to the rear of the plot, as far as possible from the street.

While protected and visibly impenetrable by day, at night the sense of duality returns, as internal light levels rise in the twilight hours to transform the house into an illuminated beacon, revealing much more about the life that exists within.

1 Home or substation? Lattice House presents a composition that challenges perceptions of scale and use.

1

Lattice House

3

2, 3 In its setting, the house gives little
away, hiding behind five full-height
jettied screens.

Lattice House

4

4–6 Throughout the day, Lattice House begins to reveal more, as daylight fades and the presence of internal lighting intensifies.

5

6

Lattice House

7

8

9

7–9 Internally, the house presents
a more familiar series of rooms
and spaces, while maintaining its
relationship with rich colours and
distinctive, finely detailed timber
screens.

Lattice House

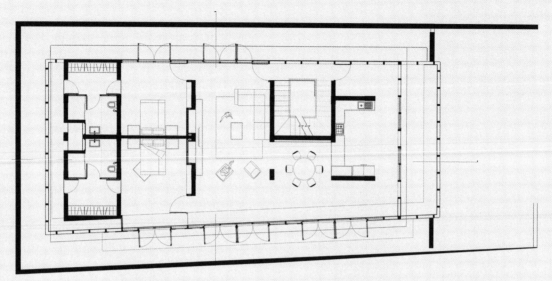

10

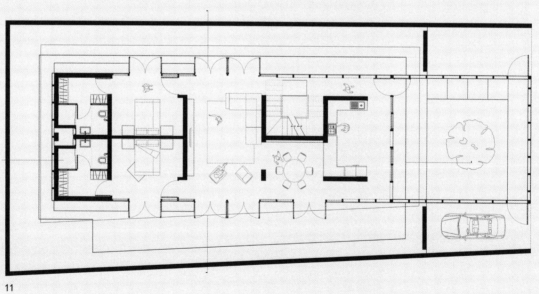

11

10, 11 Floor plans

Urban Living

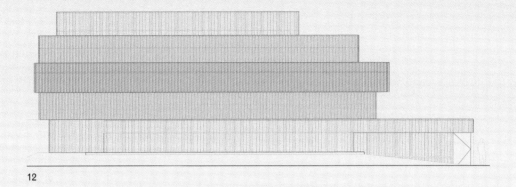

12

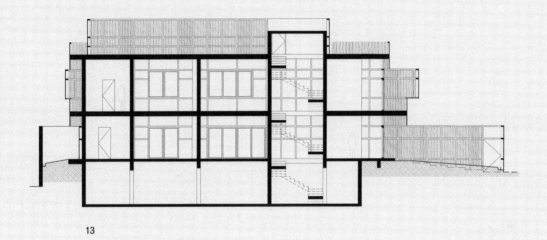

13

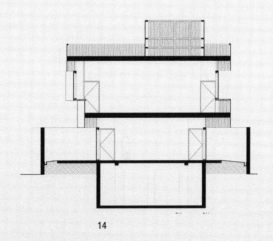

14

12–14 Sections

Lattice House

House of Secret Gardens
Ahmedabad, Gujarat
Spasm Design

'As seamless extensions of the living spaces, the gardens will mature over the years as view boxes that come alive with the moving sun, breezes animating them and rain imbuing the home with the fresh scent of the dry earth's thirst quenched.'

Spasm Design

Located in the suburbs of Ahmedabad, the House of Secret Gardens is described by its architects as an essay in Dhrangadhra stone. Mottled in texture and ivory in colour, the material was an obvious choice, locally sourced in a range of states – blocks, slabs and dust – from a nearby quarry. Its continuity brings distinction to its architecture, recalling the patina of many local antiquities, while supporting the architectural ambition to create a bold and contemporary stone monolith.

Arranged as two intersecting wings, the form of the house supports the architects' second ambition – to deliver a home that allows its occupants to live a life in the bosom of nature, in touch with the seasons, with space to entertain family and friends. The use of stone extends beyond the reach of the primary wings as a series of garden and boundary walls to bring a sense of containment and scale to the entire plot. These walls feature solid stone steps, which bring additional gravitas to the treatment of the gardens, while providing access to the more exposed roof gardens and terraces.

The narrow plan depth and correspondingly direct access to external space enriches the experience of walking through the house, with frequent glimpses of inside and out. This arrangement also helps to facilitate the movement of air through the living spaces – essential, given the region's extremely high temperatures. The building's form also responds to Ahmedabad's sharp sunlight, with cantilevers creating sheltered courtyards and verandas, which also provide protection and refuge during the monsoon season. At a finer grain, the manner in which the stone cladding has been detailed on the elevated and cantilevered wings also responds to the qualities of light, with rough-cut stone fins casting dynamic shadows on the otherwise smooth and luminous expanses of stone.

Interiors are embellished with fine metal detailing and rich joinery, with boxes containing wardrobes and large, luxurious en-suite bathrooms, which sit as discrete elements within the backdrop of ceilings and walls rendered in a stucco-like lime plaster. Both internal and external spaces are further articulated by specially commissioned pieces of furniture and works of art, including a life-sized sculpture of a pensive monk, shaped in the dark hues of Beslana stone and poised as if levitating on the surface of the tranquil water court.

1 The House of Secret Gardens uses boundary walls and cantilevered forms to create a rich variety of gardens, external rooms and interstitial spaces.

1

House of Secret Gardens

2

Urban Living

2 The cruciform plan extends into
a series of ground-floor boundary
walls that define the four principal
external gardens.

House of Secret Gardens

3

Urban Living

4

3 Stone is used in plane and on
edge, combining to create deeper
relief in elevation.
4 The ground and roof planes are
also given relief, with subtle changes
in material and level.

House of Secret Gardens

5

6

Urban Living

7

5–7 The orchestration of space celebrates the transition from outside to in, with graceful external stairs, variations in hard-, soft- and water-based landscape features, generous overhangs and dynamic screened interiors.

9

8, 9 Boundaries continue to blur in spaces like this, where existing trees are retained as centrepieces to what appear to be internal rooms.

House of Secret Gardens

10

10–12 Fine details extend throughout
the house, with many pieces of bespoke
furniture and fully integrated fixtures
and fittings.

11

12

House of Secret Gardens

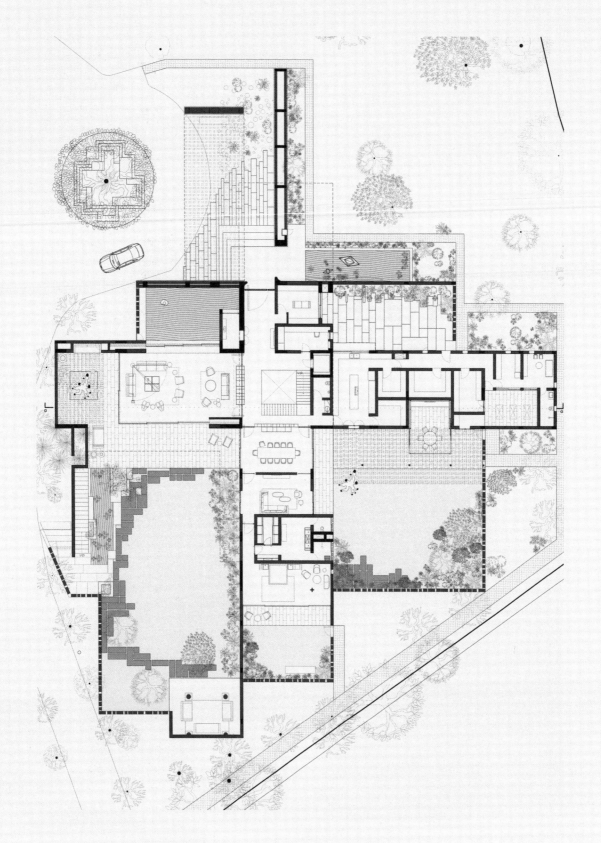

13

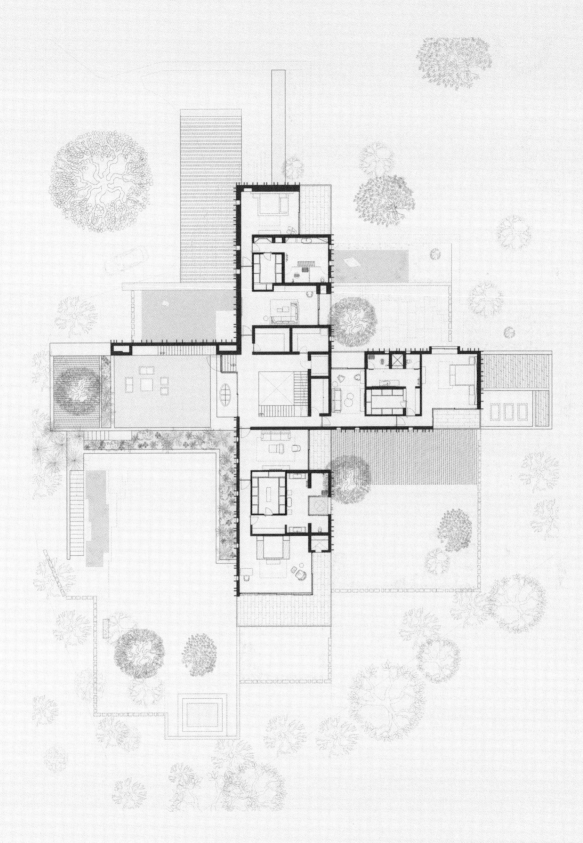

14

13 Ground-floor plan
14 First-floor plan

House of Secret Gardens

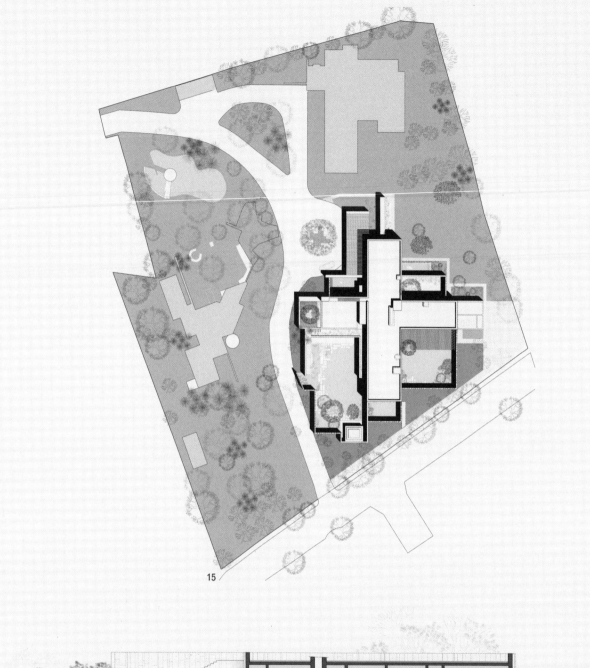

15

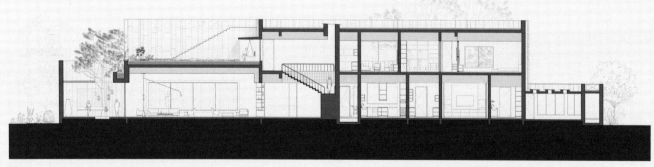

16

15 Site plan
16 Section

Urban Living

Two

Remote Villas

Remote Living:
Maintaining skills while
changing attitudes

Featured project
Belavali House
Kalyan-Dombivli, Maharashtra
Studio Mumbai

For those who can afford it, one way of coping with the challenges of urban life is to relocate to a rural retreat – whether as part of a family's permanent home or, as is more common, as a weekend retreat. In the latter, we find both the small basic home and examples of larger, multi-generational dwellings. Common across all types is the opportunity to engage with expansive landscapes and the wildlife within them.

When we began our exploration into Indian architecture, much time was spent with Bijoy Jain of Studio Mumbai, an emerging talent then based in a forest plantation in the Alibag region. With an office in Mumbai, Jain's daily commute was a privileged one, darting across the harbour in the Arabian Sea by speedboat. This gave him a deep understanding of the contrasting demands between urban and rural architecture, and he seemed equally at home with the density of the city and the tranquillity of his woodland workshop, where he had a team of over 100 skilled individuals who were maintaining the tradition and craft of the handmade home.

Craft is not the only quality of this approach, however, as a deeper understanding of nature also shines through – of both place and of people, which is important when trying to help anchor new lifestyles within their specific landscape settings. This results in homes that are undeniably of their place, both in relation to the people and the processes. We spent time with Jain both in his workshop and at Belavali House, learning about what it takes from both architect and client to co-create a new family home. While walking though the terraces and trees that surround and enclose the house, Jain observed, with a knowing sense of frustration: 'What is amazing here is that plants grow so quickly. But, unfortunately, the client keeps pruning them back.' For him, terraces don't have to be pristine. Nature is not something that has to be unfamiliar or, worse, feared.

'I am used to this environment, and understand how to live in it,' he explained. 'But it takes time to learn how to live in these landscapes and to get over the initial anxiety.' Jain and the other architects featured in this section have produced buildings that help people understand that nature, not buildings, should set the scene, without the need to tame or overcultivate the spaces that mediate between wilderness and homeliness.

'In our practice, there is no separation between artisan and architect. This generates a culture in which every part of the process is exposed and more easily shared, and everyone understands and takes their share of responsibility.'

Bijoy Jain

1

2

1, 2 Conceived as a series of
breezeway-like open pavilions,
the most private end of the building
hunkers down between existing trees
and an extended boundary wall.

Belavali House

3

4

5

3 Everything here is purpose-made,
including window frames and hinges.
4 The double-height living room
is defined by the highest quality
of polished plaster and concrete.
5 The first-floor bedroom enjoys an
elevated position among the trees
and across the immediate landscape.
6 The treatment of changes in levels
is treated with equal care.

Belavali House does this with beauty and poise, conceived as a series of naturally ventilated breezeway-like pavilions, arranged to take up as little of the land as possible. Set out on a 5 m (16 ft)-deep linear plan, which forms the eastern edge of the plot, the home is essentially single aspect, with three individual pavilions built hard up against a series of solid basalt retaining and boundary walls, which crank to negotiate their place between the site's mature mango trees. On the inner face, these walls are rendered with a polished plaster that seamlessly joins the polished concrete floor slabs. Sheltered by simple horizontal roofs, the elevations addressing the immediate and broader landscape are formed by a combination of glass and timber walls that, through beautifully crafted mechanisms, can be opened or slid away to control the relationship between inside and out.

Crucially, the architecture does not stop here, but extends out with a series of carefully moderated landscape buffers, both natural and manmade. So while stretching the accommodation along one boundary helps to give each space a unique relationship with the natural setting, it is the further elongation of architectural space that helps create those all-important thresholds and interstitial spaces between inside and out. As is evident in many of the houses featured in this chapter, it is the architect's control of the building envelope that is key to a home's ability to successfully settle into its natural setting, and crucially the place where the occupant's senses are most challenged.

6

Belavali House

7 Built close to a heavy retaining wall, the house sets up subtle geometrical shifts and creates clear thresholds between front and back.
8 Passing through the retaining wall and beneath the first-floor accommodation, the building reveals its more open façades.
9 The most public end of the house is expressed as a lofty space and open terrace, where boundaries between inside and out are at their most minimal.

7

8

9

Remote Villas

1

Wood House

Wood House
Satkhol, Uttarakhand
Matra Architects

The bold silhouette of Wood House encapsulates the architects' belief that structure can express qualities relating to the terrain on which it sits, and that the resolution of structure is how buildings communicate ideas. In its most elemental reading, the house can be surmised as a trio of stone terraces, sitting beneath a simple timber frame. The experience in context, however, is much more dramatic, layered and complex.

Located in isolation and set against a dramatic Himalayan backdrop, visitors approach from high level, zig-zagging along an open trail. The angular roofline is the first evidence of habitation, and the building presents itself as a modest, single-storey dwelling. Closer still, as the mountainous horizon disappears behind the timber-clad form, the relationship between terrace and frame, ground and sky, is articulated by the front door, which expands the junction between this dual mode of construction.

All is calm again as one contemplates the relationship between the ground-bearing, randomly coursed stone walls and the wooden cladding, stained black with engine oil. Upon entering the house, the drama of the external landscape returns in microcosm, as a spacious internal terrain of stone terraces and structural layers, set up a series of internal horizons that open out before you.

To the right, at the summit of this internal landscape, is the kitchen, which has a commanding position on the uppermost terrace, pleasingly compressed beneath the low point of the open truss roof. To the left, within one of four bedrooms, the roof soars to its heavenly high point, the rooflight concealed from view but signalled by the generous daylight and morning sun streaming in from the east. Straight ahead, the terraces drop away, perpendicular to the fall of the roof, to imply an invisible but dynamic diagonal axis as the space opens up to the centre and right.

The apparent naivety of its pitched-roof form belies the complexity of the spaces created. Correspondingly, the simplicity of its construction makes light of the mammoth task that building in such a remote setting involves. With both water and skills in scarce supply, elementary building techniques were all that were available. But through the simple superimposition of truss and terrace, and the incremental adjustments necessary from bay to bay, carpentry and masonry have produced the most delightful series of architectural outcomes, most notably with the array of diagonal truss posts fanning out as the ground falls away to the north.

1 (previous page) Wood House gains much of its character from the layering of wood on stone, and through the subtle variation of detailing therein.
2 The architects have articulated the detail between stone and wood with a continuous slot that opens up further to form the home's main entrance.

2

Wood House

3

Remote Villas

3 In its setting, the architectural relationship between stone and timber echoes the site's breathtaking panorama, as dramatic mountain peaks rise from the low-lying foothills.

Wood House

4

Remote Villas

5

4 As the roof and terraces are set out in opposing orientations, the geometry of the exposed trusses opens out as they step down the hill.
5 On axis with the main entrance, the house creates its own landscape, with the kitchen at the summit, casual seating at the base, and more formal dining somewhere in between.

Wood House

6

Remote Villas

7

8

6 As the heart of the home, the dining table commands a central position, set against a backdrop of integrated joinery shelving, balustrades and panelling.

7 All four bedrooms enjoy a corner location (seen here at the lowest level of the house), with views to the west and the north.

8 With framed views to the south and west, the uppermost bedroom also has the benefit of a lofty interior, opening up to the large rooflight to the east.

Wood House

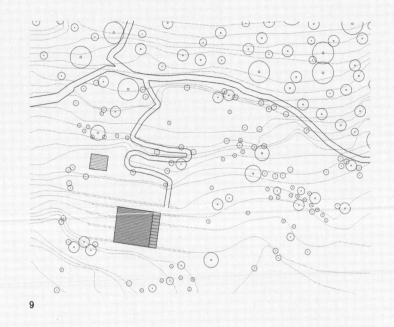

9

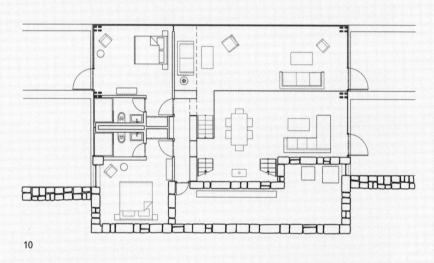

10

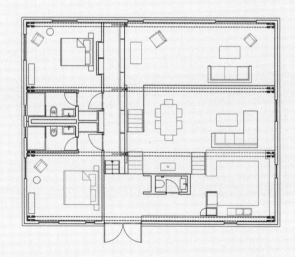

11

9, 10 Sections
11 Entrance / north elevation

Remote Villas

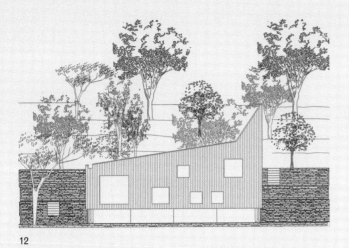

12

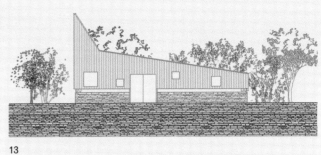

13

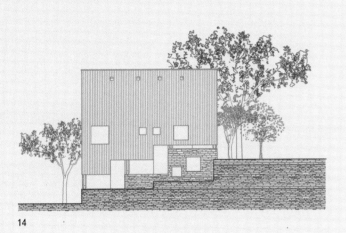

14

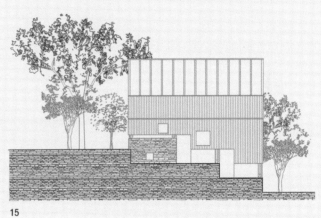

15

16

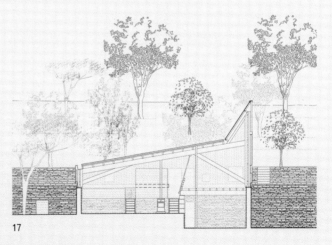

17

12 North elevation
13 South elevation
14 West elevation
15 East elevation
16 Section Y
17 Section X

Flying House
Dharamshala, Himachal Pradesh
Romi Khosla Design Studios

'Stabilized mud-brick technology is new to this part of the Himalayas. We held workshops led by Development Alternatives, a non-profit organization, to train local masons how to make bricks from the excavated earth, and several have gone on to start their own businesses.'

Martand Khosla

The design and construction of this isolated holiday home went beyond typical architectural processes, demonstrating the commitment of both architect and client to the people and place in which it is set. Located within a beautiful valley with breathtaking views of the Himalayas, the architectural ambition to create a contemporary glass pavilion may have imposed modern forms, skills and materials, but the opportunity to adopt a slower pace of construction was also pursued. Local builders were trained in contemporary construction techniques, and new technology was introduced through training workshops, enabling small groups of builders to create independent self-sustaining business models.

With a split section that sits naturally on pre-existing contours, the house comprises a number of opaque stone walls framing a series of timber-and-glass louvred panels, all of which sit beneath the building's distinctive flying roofs, which themselves provide an additional layer of shelter from both heat and rain.

The masonry superstructure combines stabilized sun-dried mud bricks with finely jointed local stone to form a series of regular bays, terraces and verandas. Into this simple opening, lights are inserted. This format allows the home to open completely to the landscape during the day, and to shut down in the evenings to create a more introverted shelter. It can also be locked down when the owners are away.

Masonry blocks avoid the use of combustible material typically required to fire traditional bricks, making them not only cheap to produce and non-polluting, but also capable of maintaining a high thermal capacity. The project achieved near-zero wastage, with off-cut stones used within the walls, broken roof tiles to form the external floors, and residual wood to make furniture and household objects.

Simple in plan and section, the accommodation includes two bedrooms and a large, open-plan kitchen, dining and living room on the upper level. Turning in to focus on a simple fireplace at night, during the day the living room is outward-looking, taking advantage of its triple aspect by opening out onto a linear terrace, which offers an incredible 200° view of the valley and the snow-capped peaks to the north, west and south. At the eastern end, the dining room and kitchen capture the morning sun, opening onto a large terrace set within a field of wild grasses, creating a natural wall of privacy for outdoor dining.

Below, as the land falls naturally away, are two additional bedrooms that open out onto a series of courtyard gardens, creating a tame foreground to the vast wilderness of the Himalayas beyond.

1 The breathtaking Himalayan landscape forms a dramatic backdrop to the house.

1

Flying House

Remote Villas

3

2 In this remote location, client and architect worked closely with the local workforce, training them in new forms of construction.
3 On approach, the simple pavilion presents a series of solid boundary walls, briefly concealing the panoramic view from visitors.

Flying House

4

5

Remote Villas

6

4 The distinctive 'flying' forms shelter
an otherwise simple flat roof from heat
and rain.
5, 6 The exposed masonry walls feature
finely joined local stone.

Flying House

7

Remote Villas

8

9

7 Working with existing contours, the
house steps down to provide space for
two additional bedrooms, each opening
onto a sunken terrace.
8, 9 The principal living room is
articulated by a simple timber-and-
glass screen, which controls ventilation
and sunlight penetration.

Flying House

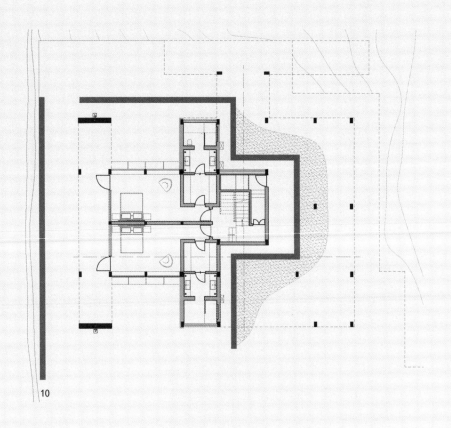

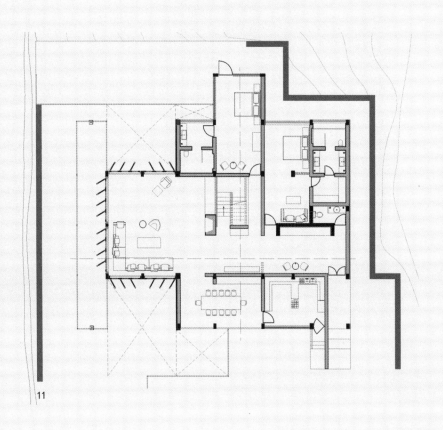

10, 11 Plans

Remote Villas

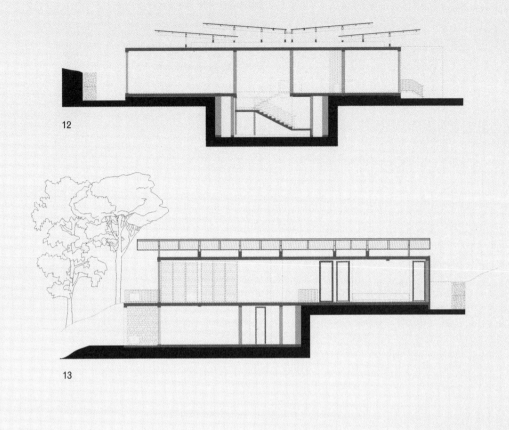

12

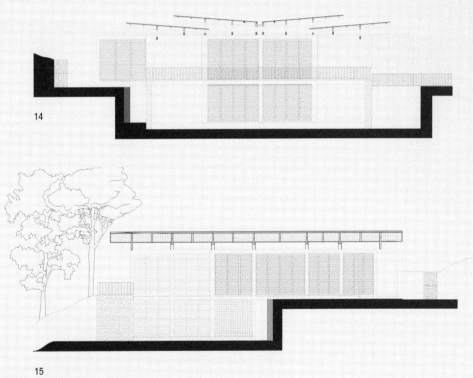

13

14

15

12–15 Sections

Flying House

House Cast in Liquid Stone
Khopoli, Maharashtra
Spasm Design

'Indian families are generally big, and they come with friends, cousins, extended family. All of these people tend to come together in the courtyard, which becomes the room for expansion.'

Spasm Design

Located in Khopoli's western highlands in Maharashtra, 70 km (43 miles) southeast of Mumbai, this house, known as the House Cast in Liquid Stone, exploits the duality of its position, poised as it is at the top of a rocky basalt outcrop. Built to provide a relaxing weekend home for a Mumbai-based businessman and his family, it presents an imposing face, with the 30 m (98 ft)-long fortress-like principal wall giving little away as to what lies beyond. Low-lying and completely unadorned, distant views are deliberately blocked and there are no signs of life or hospitality.

Once inside, however, having passed beneath a series of impressive and audacious concrete cantilevers, essential for protecting visitors who arrive during the monsoon, the home opens up into a series of inviting, warmly furnished and intimately scaled internal and external spaces. As deep as the primary wall is long, the hidden interiors lead family and guests into areas that frame commanding and extensive views of the flatlands and mountains beyond.

Breaking down the form of what appears monolithic and singular, the house opens out into a labyrinth of modern caves. Three principal courtyards, built around a number of existing mango trees, are cut into the plan of the house, bringing light and air deep into the heart of the home and creating focal points for the main living space, three bedrooms and the kitchen. Below this, stepping down the face of the escarpment, is another bedroom.

The use of concrete with local aggregate brings continuity between the basalt bedrock and the new cast walls. Elsewhere, other types of stone maintain the sense of gravitas while providing complementary alternative surfaces, from highly polished stone floors in the principal living spaces, across rougher flagstones that extend out into the landscape, as strips that reach out into areas of gravel.

But these hard masonry surfaces have been softened by nature, with plants and grasses repossessing the courtyards. Trees continue to grow freely, and even the concrete is beginning to be taken over by climbing plants. An external bathroom maximizes the benefit of this blurring of boundaries between nature and the manmade, heightening the experience of bathing, reclining under a mango tree and surrounded by floating marigolds. Timber fit-out and brightly coloured furniture are added to produce a surprisingly informal modern house that hides a traditional courtyard house plan behind a dominant concrete wall.

1 Cast in concrete (or 'liquid stone'), the house assumes a cavernous quality, with spaces taking on a robust, monolithic character.

1

House Cast in Liquid Stone

2

Remote Villas

2 On approach, the house features a generous sheltered arrivals space, providing only brief glimpses of what lies beyond.

House Cast in Liquid Stone

3

4

5

3 The entrance canopy yields to
one of several retained mango trees
at the point where visitors turn and
enter the house.
4 A sliding screen animates the
threshold between inside and out.
5 The main living space maintains
the expression of cast concrete,
complemented by brightly coloured,
homely furniture.

House Cast in Liquid Stone

6

Remote Villas

6 The living area sits between two
courtyards, one of which provides
access onto the expansive flat roof.

House Cast in Liquid Stone

8

9

7, 8 The second principal courtyard
features an infinity pool, which helps
to frame views across the flatlands
and mountains beyond.
9 As the house projects out over
the rocky outcrop, space is used at
the lower level to provide a private
and more intimate bedroom suite.

House Cast in Liquid Stone

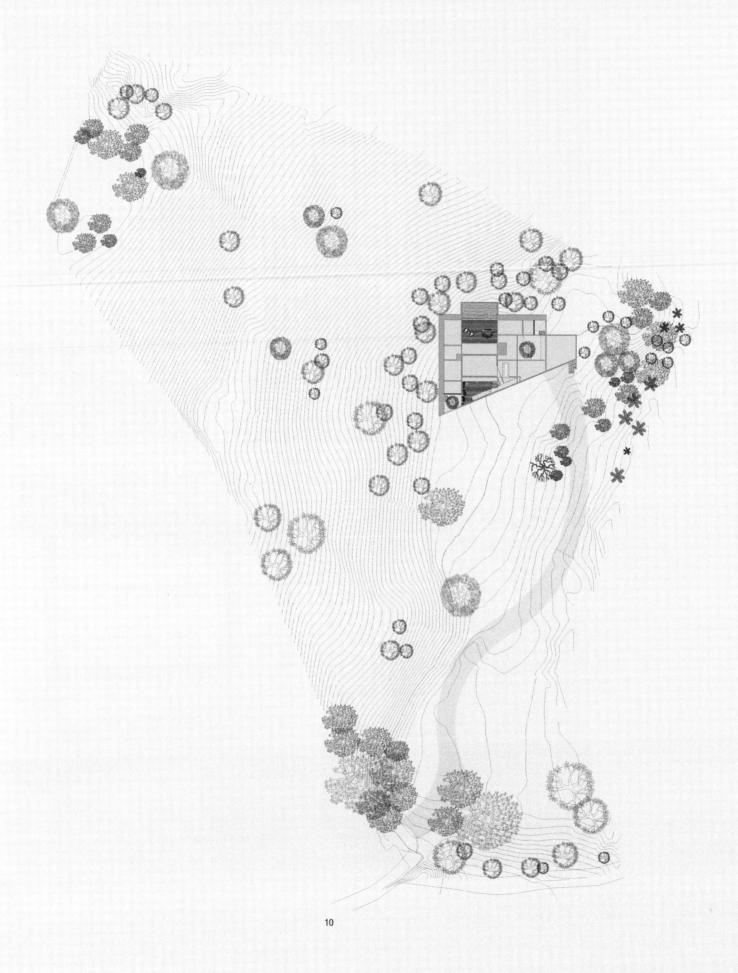

10

10–12 Plans

Remote Villas

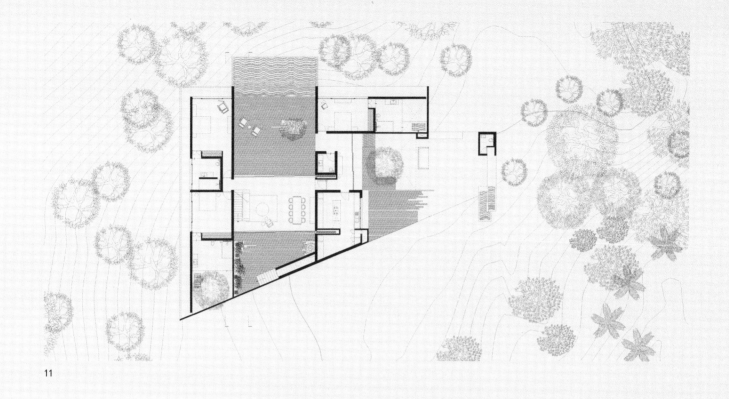

11

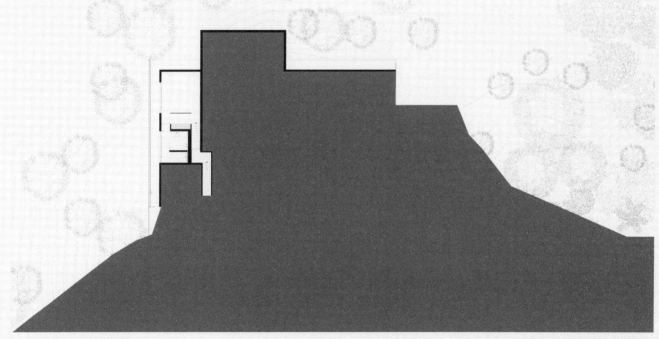

12

House Cast in Liquid Stone

Retreat in Sahyadris
Maharashtra
Khosla Associates

'We had to exercise a great deal of restraint in the furniture and accessories, customizing each piece to be in harmony with the architectural intent.'

Sandeep Khosla

The overall intent of this retreat is expressed by three key architectural moves: a box sitting on a plinth; a hovering roof protecting it from sun and rain; and random apertures admitting soft light within. These were made in response to the house's dramatic setting, perched above a large lake and surrounded by the Western Ghats mountain range (known as 'Sahyadri') in Maharashtra.

The architecture also responds to the clients' brief, which, despite owning two acres of land, focused on the relatively modest request for a single-storey weekend retreat of 195 m² (2,100 sq ft). The primary objective was to build a home that would offer respite from their busy Mumbai lives, and to this end the house maximizes the characteristics of the site by hunkering down at the most elevated position at the top of the plot.

Subtle level changes on this relatively flat section of land have been incorporated into a sunken entrance court, which contains a garage and, at a slightly lower level, an intimate courtyard garden, accessible from the bedrooms. Beyond this, a simple plinth extends out towards the expansive panoramic views, onto which the main pavilion is placed.

The living accommodation is broken down into two distinct areas. To the east, benefiting from the shelter of the sunken courtyards, are two bedroom suites – one with shower and children's spaces, the other with a more generous bathroom. To the west are the principal living spaces, commanding extensive views with direct access on three sides to decks, seating areas and an infinity pool. The landscape beyond is left unmanicured, with large and small rocks, low shrubbery and carefully planted fruit trees, reinforcing the existing terrain in an attempt to bring the built form closer to nature.

While distinct in function and outlook, both private and communal spaces share the same floor and roof, with each horizontal plane finished in fine Kota stone and polished cement plaster, respectively. Accents of articulation are provided by plywood panels, which rise up to frame a series of north-facing rooflights. Internally, these elements bring warmth and generosity to key spaces – hallway, bathrooms, living room and kitchen – while externally, they articulate the otherwise horizontal composition to mimic the profile of the mountain peaks defining horizons to the east and west.

Additional accents and points of articulation include the black basalt walls, windows handcrafted in Accoya wood, and carefully chosen accessories, including brass and copper vessels from Nashik and Bidriware from Bidar.

1 Sharp manmade lines complement the stunning natural forms of the Sahyadri mountain range.

1

Retreat in Sahyadris

2

3

Remote Villas

4

5

2 On approach, a series of angular
rooflights create their own rocky
silhouette.
3, 4 Boundary walls, a projecting roof
and framed views combine to animate
the approach to the front door.
5 Glimpsed through the screen wall,
a semi-private terrace sits beneath
a framework of steel.

Retreat in Sahyadris

6

7

Remote Villas

8

9

6, 7 The main living space flows freely
onto the pool terrace, while a series of
finely made timber-and-glass screens
fold and slide.
8, 9 The interiors feature a restrained
palette of rich materials, with timber
linings to the projecting rooflights
and simple timber furniture.

Retreat in Sahyadris

10

11

12

10–12 Timber, stone, glass, polished plaster and concrete bring a consistent quality to the internal spaces, including passageways, and dining and living areas.

Retreat in Sahyadris

13

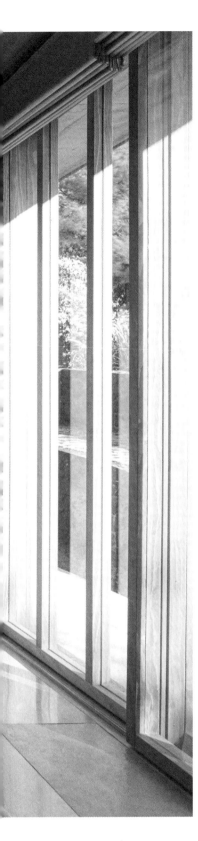

14

13, 14 Bedrooms and bathrooms
provide privacy, while maintaining the
material quality of the communal space,
using the junction between wall and
roof to bring additional moments of
articulation.

Retreat in Sahyadris

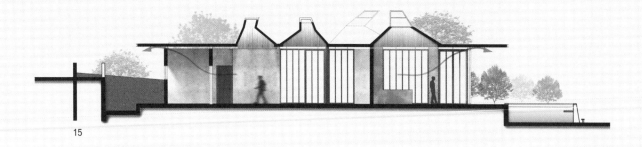

15

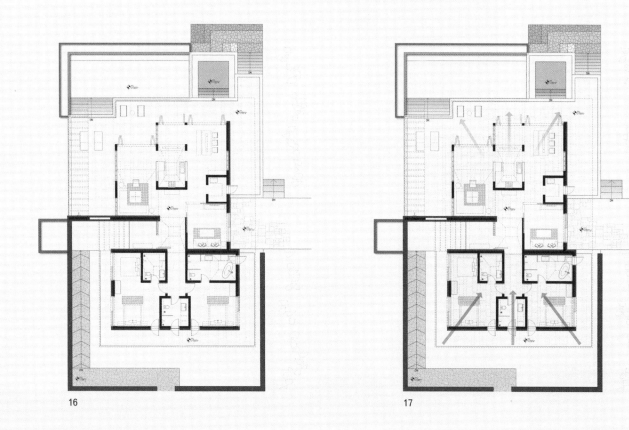

16   17

15 Section
16, 17 Plans
18 Site plan

Remote Villas

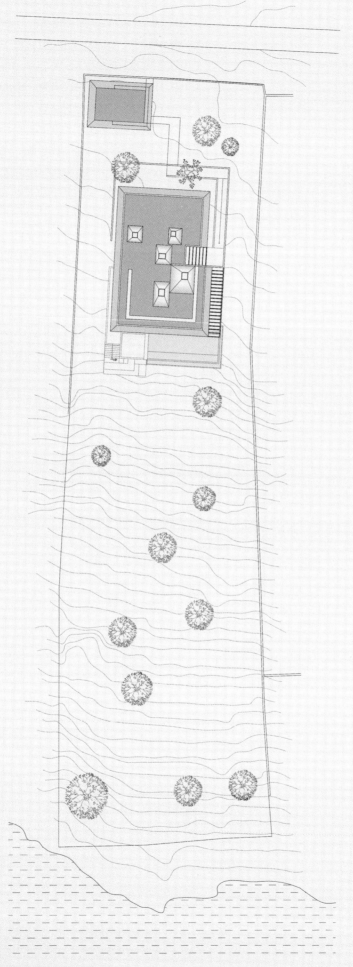

Tala Treehouse Villa
Kuda, Maharashtra
Architecture Brio

'We wanted to emphasize the horizontal openness beneath the dominant roof and use as few materials as possible, including minimal framing for windows to soften the edges of each enclosure. This helps give twilight reflections an illusory quality, playing with depth and orientation, and inside and out.'

Robert Verrijt

The opportunity to complete what was a partially built treehouse allowed the architects to explore further their interest in the relationship between established architectural typologies and a range of unique landscape settings. The 160-acre site is just a stone's throw from the Kuda Caves, where Buddhist monks made their home over two thousand years ago. The landscape is recognized for its unique and meditative qualities, and this small holiday home allows up to six people to come here and to enjoy its presence.

With roof and stilts already in place, working with and blending the archetypes of hut and tent, the architects set about re-imagining the interior through the creation of a series of new domestic spaces, each with different levels of transparency and enclosure.

Located on the crest of a hill, about 200 m (656 ft) above an estuary, the house reveals itself as visitors move through the forest and across meadows of seasonal mustard plants, with the distinctive roof silhouette slowly coming into focus. Crossing a timber bridge onto a large stilted deck, the route wraps around the house and culminates in an expansive and open viewing platform, which projects out from beneath the tree.

Upon turning inside, visitors are met by a composition of partly reflective surfaces, which animate and enliven the space, re-interpreting notions of domesticity, privacy and exposure. The upper level, conceived as a single space, includes three distinct enclosures for the master bedroom, bathroom and pantry. A bed deck sits above the latter, with a spiral stair leading to a more private bedroom suite, which hangs below, suspended among the trunks and branches. Space flows between these areas, maintaining the sense of openness and connections to the landscape beyond.

Throughout the project, the architects described their approach as one that embraces nature, accepting its character and taking on its challenges. There was no attempt to domesticate nature, nor have they attempted to 'naturalize' architecture. Instead, they searched for just the right amount of confrontation, establishing equilibrium between natural processes and architectural permanence, creating a stage from which to experience place and time.

1 Inserted beneath an existing thatched roof, this new holiday home features steel, timber, fabric and mirrored glass.
2 Where additional space was required, new decks and enclosures were created, delicately finding their place between existing trunks and branches.

1

2

Tala Treehouse Villa

3

4

3, 4 A simple spiral stair drops down
to a second bedroom suite, suspended
beneath the main deck.
5 The principal space is articulated
by curtains that allow different spatial
configurations to be simply created.
6 The lower bedroom hangs within
the lower reaches of the tree canopies.

Remote Villas

5

6

Tala Treehouse Villa

7

8

7 Taking advantage of the lofty
thatched roof, the main space includes
a mezzanine positioned above a service
pod.
8 The external bathroom sits within
a mirrored glass screen, sharing space
with sizable trunks and branches.

Tala Treehouse Villa

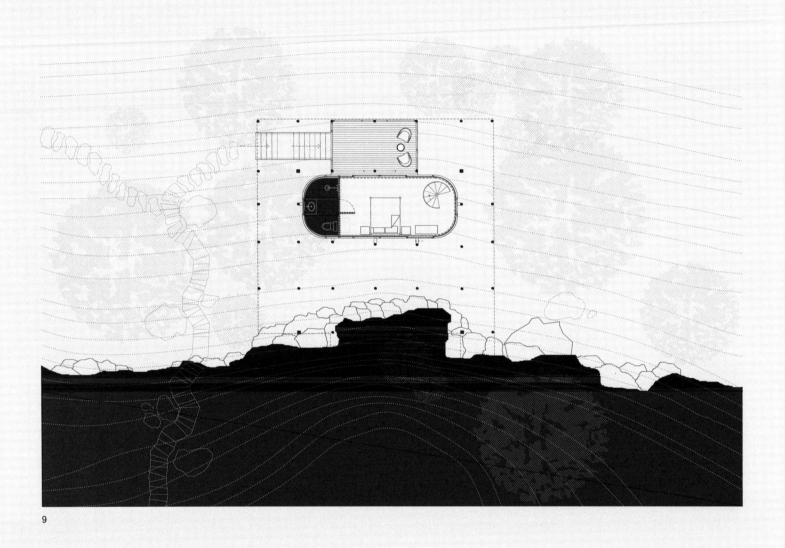

9

9, 10 Plans

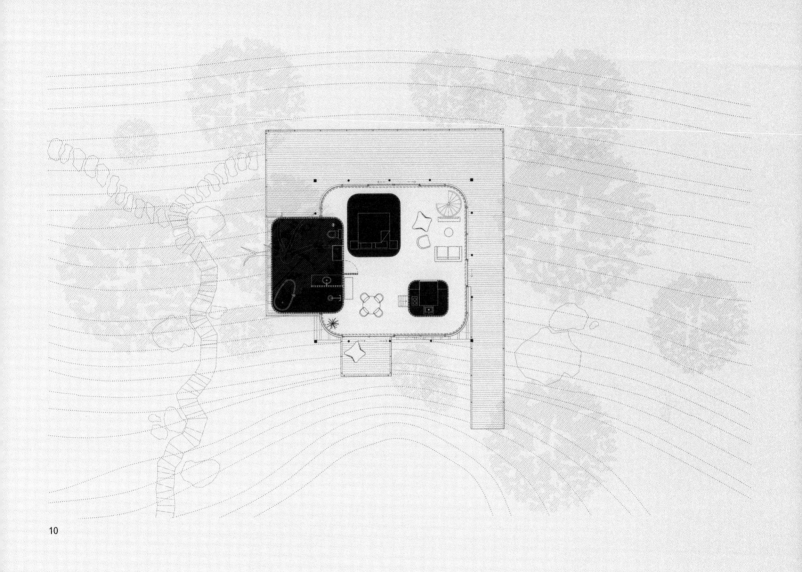

10

Tala Treehouse Villa

11

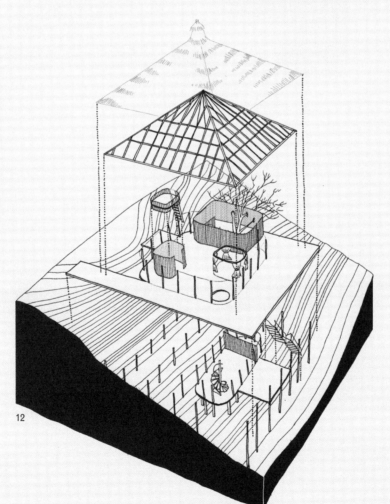

12

11, 12 Sections

Remote Villas

Three

New
Settlements

New Settlements:
Spaces and places

Featured project

Broacha House
Alibag, Maharashtra
Samira Rathod Design Associates

Whereas the single house tends to impose a new and consolidated figure into its setting, be that urban or rural, another architectural response to large rural sites is to break down the building into numerous individual parts, using their disposition and interrelationship to create new forms of settlement. In doing so, previously undeveloped land can gain a more meaningful and habitable structure, as manmade boundaries and buildings combine to create distinct internal and external areas of open space.

Broacha House exemplifies this approach, and demonstrates how architecture can make sense of the otherwise nondescript farmland that is typically parcelled up and sold off as development plots. Often featureless, with one or two trees – or a well, if you're lucky – the seasons and climate frequently become the most dynamic elements for architects and clients to respond to. Speaking about the relationship between her client and her design, Samira Rathod explains: 'In this region, it rains for two months of the year. We then get three months of vivid green landscape, followed by seven months of a more muted brown. So it's no surprise that my client, who is a photographer, essentially wanted to live outdoors, so that she could make the most of the experience of living within this expansive and changing landscape.'

In response, Rathod designed the house as a series of outdoor rooms that exploit the region's cooling breeze, reducing reliance on power-thirsty air-conditioning. This permeable approach to planning creates what she describes as a stage set, 'where you sense that everything can move or shift and change'. Nothing looks like it is here to stay, so landscape is king. A real sense of place, however, is also somehow magically achieved.

With this kind of settlement-based approach, walking is essential. When moving around the site, it becomes reminiscent of an informal settlement or camp – in this case, centred around an external living area that sits beneath a generous, pitched cement canopy. This open, sheltered space forms the heart of the house, linking kitchen and dining spaces to

'This house is about wellbeing and how light and air come into the space. I believe that spaces and places can define a person's life, thinking and personal growth.'

Samira Rathod

1, 2 Broacha House takes the from of
an encampment, with a large, marquee-
like sheltered space, adjacent to an
open pool.

1

2

3

4

5

New Settlements

3–5 Around the edges of the base
camp, the house includes a variety
of structures, including an elevated
bridge, a pavilion-like sitting room
and a simple canopy.
6 Built for a photographer, the house
features a number of playful elements,
including these lens-like apertures.

6

the left with three bedrooms and studio above and to the right. Bridges and stairs link the two-storey volumes, implying a degree of privacy from the otherwise free-flow terrain of open land, terraces and sheltered living rooms. This is an animated composition in which spatial freedom is more palpable than any sense of containment, providing a contrast to the client's experience of living and working in Mumbai, a commute that is easily manageable from Alibag with its regular boat services and water taxis.

Rathod remembers with pride how she won the job by demonstrating her clear enthusiasm for the recently acquired plot of land. 'When my client first bought the site,' she explains, 'a number of other architects declined the commission, as they thought it was an uninspiring piece of land. But when we visited it together, my response was, "wow, this is great". It seemed I was the first architect to like it.'

Happy to let her ideas take seed, and to gain a greater understanding of the land and its climate, Rathod plans to enhance the landscape by planting a grove of frangipani trees and tall grass, as privacy becomes necessary from adjacent developments. This is a necessary skill for architects who take on sites like this – to see beyond the barren and featureless foreground, to restructure land previously demarcated by a simple wire boundary, and to imagine the rich, dynamic life that comes through the changing seasons and weather patterns. The houses in this section have all adopted similar approaches to create single and multi-generational homes, demonstrating the influence that architecture can have on landscape and place-making.

Broacha House

7, 8 Bedrooms are perhaps the most familiar room types in this house, located in a number of detached two-storey blocks.
9 Architect and client have long-term plans to cultivate the landscape that surrounds and weaves its way between each new built element.

7

8

9

New Settlements

Villa in the Palms
Penha de França, Goa
Abraham John Architects

'Being builders themselves, the clients wanted to build cheap. The first thing they asked was how we could build more and save money. With the trees, working with the restrictions, rather than an empty canvas, was so much better.'

Abraham John

This new settlement gives uncompromising primacy to nature, preserving as it does twenty 18 m (60 ft)-high, fifty-year-old coconut trees. The architect-led commitment was no mean feat to deliver, as the client originally wanted two houses on the site, and wasn't at all precious about preserving the trees. Balancing persuasion with technical competence, while taking a bit of a punt on the trees' resilience, the architectural vision is fulfilled in what we see before us today: a 450 m² (4,844 sq ft) four-bedroom holiday home in the coastal state of Goa, which threads its way between the trees to form three self-contained guest suites, along with extensive communal living areas and an elevated master suite.

Building the house required a degree of delicacy not commonly associated with groundworks packages, as a team of contractors followed the setting-out lines that had been marked out between the trees. In places where pools and other below-ground services were planned, the substructure was up to 1.5 m (5 ft) deep, leaving root cubes around each trunk held within crisp retaining walls of reinforced concrete.

Once safely out of the ground, the client, who was also the builder, was in more familiar territory, and went on to construct a series of conjoined pavilions, which strike a pleasing balance between traditional and contemporary. Local stone and timber combine with the universality of steel and glass to create a muted palette of materials, and shallow pitched roofs in an array of orientations form silhouettes that recall the image of village settlements, which would be familiar to local residents. The solid stone walls provide privacy, and set up sightlines across the plot, over a seasonal stream that borders the site, and onto the expansive landscape of the neighbouring field.

Accessed from the east, passing through a full-height boundary wall, visitors are presented with a westerly view across a deck on to the pool, which cuts across the full width of the site. To the right is a living-room pavilion, pinned to the land by a tree that penetrates its roof, and to the left are the main communal spaces, including dining room, kitchens and staff accommodation. Following the axial view, crossing the bridge and passing beneath the first-floor master suite, guests first encounter the sheltered wet-bar area, before being led on to one of three guest suites, each of which enjoys a balance of communality and privacy with its own front garden, internal courtyard, bathroom courtyard and rear garden. They combine to form a village of villas, with each finding its own unique place.

1 (previous page), 2 In elevation and plan view, the proximity of house and tree is clear to see, on a site where twenty or so mature palm trees were carefully retained.

2

Villa in the Palms

3

New Settlements

3 The retention of so many mature trees gives the impression that these recently completed homes have been here for many years.

Villa in the Palms

4

5

New Settlements

6

4 On approach, the house is contained within a series of solid boundary walls.
5 Where necessary, existing trees are integrated within the new structures.
6 Concrete tree pits are incorporated into a new pool to ensure the existing plants are protected and nourished.

Villa in the Palms

7

8

New Settlements

9

7 A new pool extends to an existing ha-ha, while providing separation between communal and private areas.
8, 9 A poolside bar and entertainment space creates a threshold space between social and sleeping spaces.

Villa in the Palms

10

11

New Settlements

12

10 As individual units, each bedroom suite has its own entrance.
11 Masonry, steel and timber together create a coherent palette of materials.
12 Each bedroom suite includes its own external bathroom enclosure.

Villa in the Palms

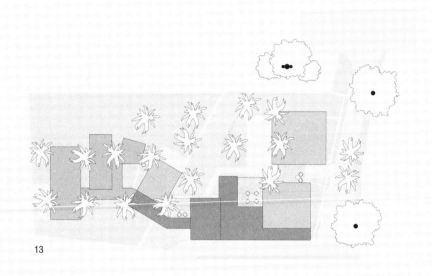

13

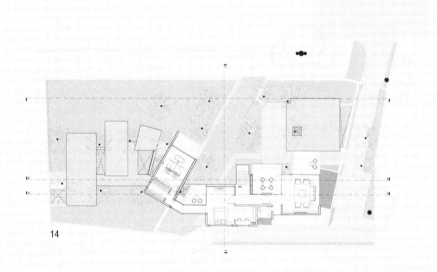

14

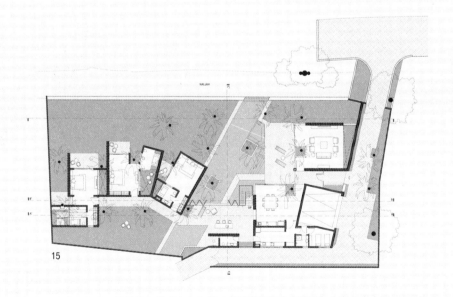

15

13–15 Plans

New Settlements

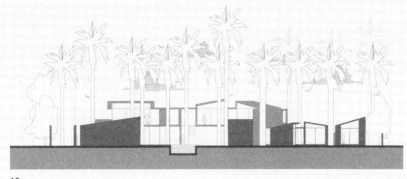

16

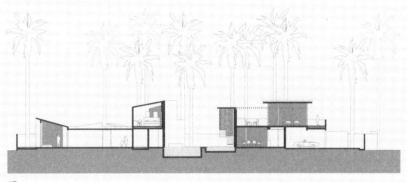

17

18

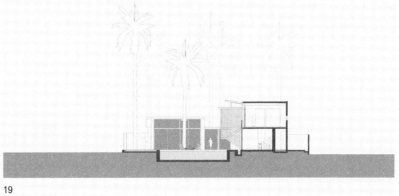

19

16 Elevation
17–19 Sections

Villa in the Palms

House on a Stream
Alibag, Maharashtra
Architecture Brio

'Who says buildings need to be pretty? We don't ask it of paintings, novels or films, so why do we ask it of architecture? Doing so highlights the contradiction between architecture and nature. For us, the pleasure is not in the denial, but in the collision between man and nature.'

Robert Verrijt

House on a Stream creates a new settlement that exploits the stark differences existing between India's dry and monsoon seasons. Conceived as two houses with the landscape in between, it straddles a rocky stream belt that zig-zags across the site. By breaking up the house in this way, not only do the landscape and seasonal river become more present, taking centre stage, it also brings a dynamism to everyday life, as the occupants move between principal living areas and the more isolated master bedroom suite.

This separation and distance in plan is also evident in section, as the building's concrete figures are chipped away, like rocks in a stream, to produce angular forms the architect likens to abandoned concrete bunkers, strewn on a beach, which are somehow both alien and familiar in their natural setting. This serves to further reduce the footprint and impact on the land, and heightens the articulation of nature and the manmade.

Further articulation is achieved by cantilevering the master bedroom above the water. Raising it above the landscape paradoxically heightens the room's connection to it. Similarly, the living room is 1.5 m (5 ft) above ground – at strategic positions, elevated penetrations in the heavy concrete walls frame specific elements of the site through contrasting glass bay windows, framed externally in galvanized steel and plywood.

The fair-faced concrete exteriors that playfully contrast with the white-painted interior heighten the notion of duality. Unlike the traditional vernacular, where material continuity is common between inside and out, the house decouples the external and internal forms in its volumetric expression, with the internal lining following its own profile by changing the relative depths of walls and ceilings. This echoes the natural duality of the place, where the dry river belt becomes a violent stream rushing around the corners during the monsoon season.

Through its composition – the path, bridge, and details like the outdoor bathroom – the house challenges the prevailing preference among Indian clients to exclude nature, despite their apparent eagerness to escape urban life and dystopian chaos. When read as a single composition, its inflections in plan and section give it an anthropomorphic quality: feeding off its surroundings, reaching out, turning corners, creating courtyards, leaping across the stream, then pausing to take a view back across it, succeeding in different ways to relate home to landscape.

1 Bunker-like concrete forms exaggerate the relationship between manmade and natural in the landscape.

1

House on a Stream

2

New Settlements

2, 3 Rough-cast concrete, galvanized steel and flashes of joinery make up the limited palette of materials.

House on a Stream

4

4 Steps, inset plinths and cantilevers
create elevated levels that anticipate
the rising water of the monsoon season.
5 Simple forms nestle into pockets in
the mature landscape.
6 A covered path, pool and bridge
articulate the journey between the main
house and the master bedroom suite.

New Settlements

5

6

7

8

7, 8 In contrast to the rough-cast external surfaces, the interiors are dry-lined with plasterboard. On occasion, the internal linings shift in form to create surprising volumes of space.
9, 10 Exposed concrete provides points of accent in some internal spaces, while the bathroom is open to the elements and has concrete fully exposed.

New Settlements

9

10

　　　　　　　　　　　　　　　House on a Stream

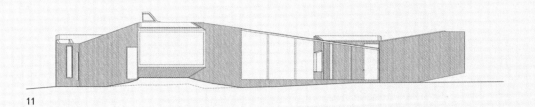

11

12

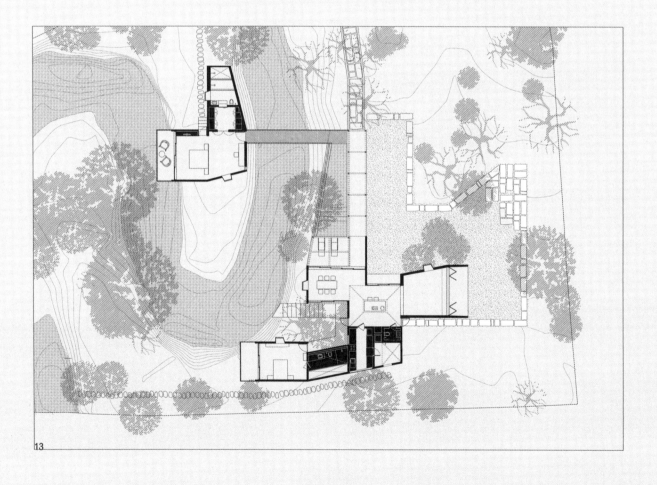

13

11, 12 Elevations
13 Site plan

14

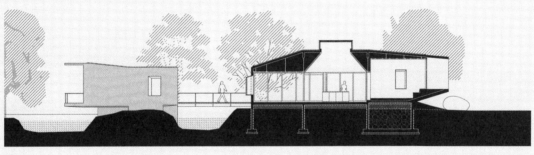

15

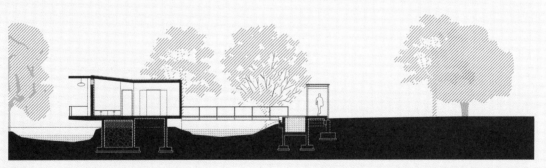

16

14–16 Sections

House on a Stream

Shadow House
Mumbai, Maharashtra
Samira Rathod Design Associates

A number of houses by the Mumbai-based architect Samira Rathod adopt a relaxed and improvised attitude to settlement, and this 465 m² (5,000 sq ft) house on the outskirts of Alibag is no exception. It can be likened to an encampment in which residents move around, where the spaces in between are as important as the home's principal rooms. This creates an arrangement of courtyards, canyons, paths and bridges, in which nature and the weather are invited to improvise in the cycles of everyday life. Taming conventional tensions between nature and the manmade, such an arrangement invites the ceaseless cycle of shadows to rise and fall in a mediating and perpetual dance, through which material gives shadow its identity, form gives shadow its depth, and structure gives shadow its pace.

The settlement found its place between two pre-existing trees, and creates identity in an otherwise barren and unforgiving landscape by presenting itself as a singular mass, articulated by concrete forms of different scale and grain. As you approach them, these concrete masses distinguish themselves further through subtle differentiations in aggregate and construction joints, and with the addition of a finer grain of timber and metal detail, which burns red in the equally unforgiving sunlight. When you finally experience it from within, the house is much more porous, opening into a series of intimate domestic spaces, rendered in warm, earthy hues, and given human scale through a syncopated timber fenestration and an enveloping and more hospitable pitched roof.

In this softer heart sits a landscaped courtyard, which sets up a strong diagonal axis connecting pool to living room and veranda beyond. Above this, accessed by an intricately detailed timber stair, is the rhythmically ordered bridge, which shelters beneath the fall of the Corten steel roof in a commanding position to link the master and children's bedrooms, which themselves occupy opposite corners of the house.

It is in this elevated space that the shadow finds its greatest liberty, cutting up the light, which enters the home's most private spaces, and creating dynamic patterns that bring the otherwise static structure to life. Reminiscent of the traditional homes of northern India, it is in this space that Rathod exerts her most inventive architectural prowess, with windows that hang like piano keys, captured mid-action. This frozen improvisation extends further in details including doors that concertina, and table legs, floor patterns and cotton sheers that overlap and create a subtle play with the shadow.

1 Shadow House combines rough-cast concrete, zinc and timber, set within a highly manicured domestic landscape.

Shadow House

1

2

3

2, 3 In seeking to give the building
presence in the landscape, the design
presents a strong, consolidated form
to the landscape, near and far.
4, 5 From within, the house is much
more open and informal, centred around
a pool and courtyard garden.

New Settlements

4

5

Shadow House

6

7

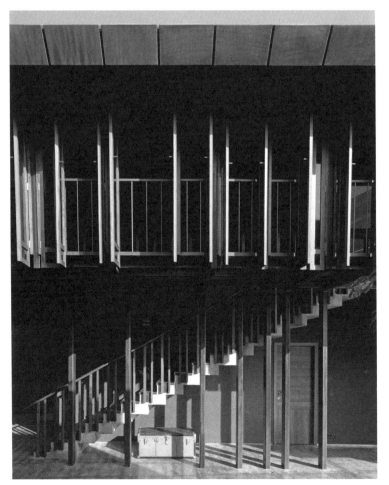

8

6–8 A stair and elevated bridge form a dominant feature at the heart of the home, highly articulated in timber and zinc.

New Settlements

9

9 Set within the elevated bridge, the
finely articulated gallery sets up myriad
optical effects, as light and shade pass
through the space.

Shadow House

10

New Settlements

11

10, 11 The principal living room is double-height, and connects directly to the plot's perimeter garden when the concertina screen is pulled away.

Shadow House

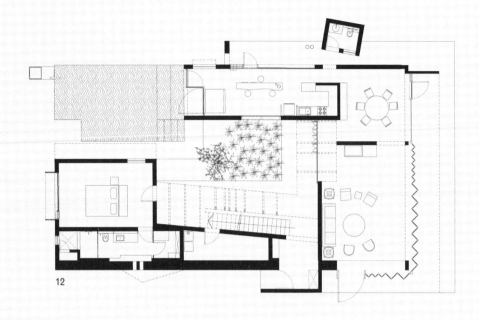

12

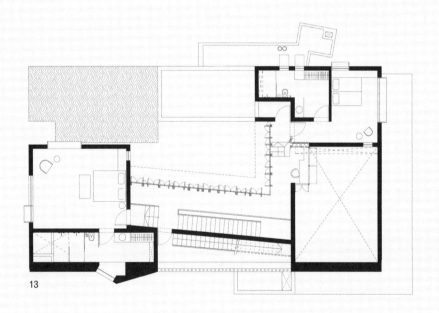

13

12, 13 Plans

New Settlements

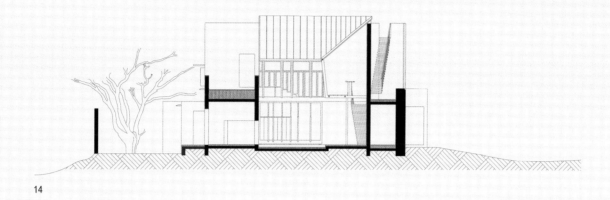

14

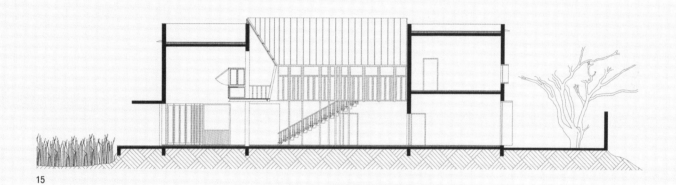

15

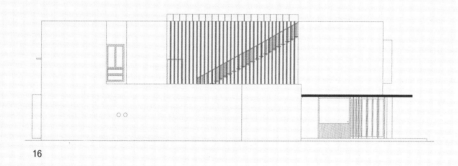

16

14, 15 Sections
16 Elevation

Shadow House

House at Alibag
Alibag, Maharashtra
Malik Architecture

'With constant shifts in geometry and plane, it was a challenge to resolve all of the details. Somehow, the landscape helps to settle the geometric complexity.'

Arjun Malik

Situated in the tropical region of Alibag, outside Mumbai, this dramatic home merges two local qualities through a response to topography and reinterpretation of traditional roof forms. Where shade was one of the most important requirements, a series of deep roofs and verandas combine in a composition that is both dynamic and calm, while decisions about where to touch the ground and where to sail over it produced a truly three-dimensional response to the steep terrain.

Anchored to the site by two vertical cores, elsewhere a series of terraced or inclined spaces break free from the land, minimizing the excavation and articulating how topography can drive the way buildings are formed. This architectural response liberates any sense of traditional formality, as spaces have been pulled apart and characterized by unique and distinctive relationships to immediate and distant features in the landscape. The fragmentation of boundaries reduces bulk, helps harness natural ventilation and encourages flow, as breezes and residents are free to navigate the site, by entering, leaving and re-entering spaces at will.

With no formal front, back or entrance, hierarchy is derived from the house's relationship to the ground, as the building is pinned to the land by a dining room at the top and a den at the bottom. In between, a series of communal and private spaces find their own place, linked by steps and bridges, and sheltered by three principal roof forms that fold in response to natural contours in section and manmade geometries in plan.

In relation to the construction, the house represents architect Arjun Malik's most experimental period of design, in which computer-aided parametric modelling tools helped resolve structural equilibrium and expression. This generated many unique junctions and details, but primarily reduced redundant structure, with each element sized according to its load, resulting in angular patterns that allow the story and making of the house to be fully revealed.

Described by Malik as an organism, the house takes on the characteristics of a creature feeding off the terrain topography and climate. 'I designed it immediately after training in New York,' he says. 'This was a very intense period of eighteen months of being bombarded with a lot of information, sitting face to face with some of the finest architects of that time. On returning to India, I had certain ideas that had to come out.'

At its core, the House at Alibag draws on a close reading of climate, nature and traditional architectural ideas. It then articulates these in an ambitious and bold new way, representing this architect's first experiment in the reinterpretation of building as a complete landscape form.

1, 2 (overleaf) As one of the most formally assertive designs in this survey, the House at Alibag merges international architectural theories with the architect's understanding of local cultural traditions.

House at Alibag

2

New Settlements

House at Alibag

3

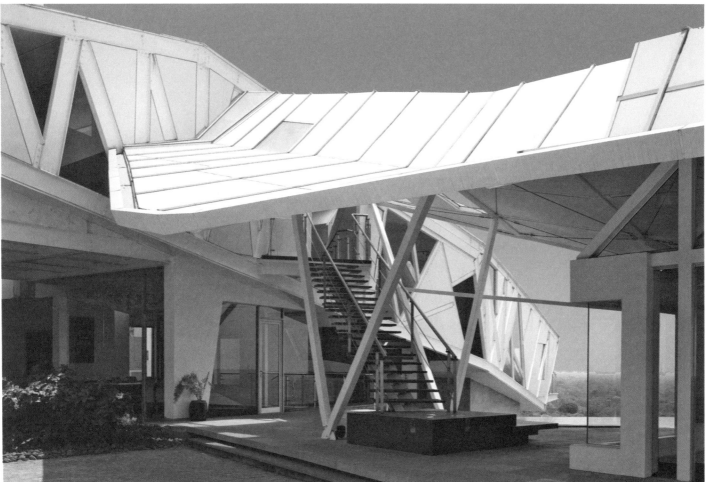

4

New Settlements

5

6

3, 4 The house has no formal front
or back, but can be approached
in the round via a series of open
terraces and verandas.
5, 6 Dramatic oversailing roofs
provide essential shelter from the
sun, and frame tranquil views of
the landscape beyond.

House at Alibag

7

8

7, 8 Each bedroom suite has its
own orientation and outlook, with
the roof extending out to shelter
and screen private verandas.
9, 10 The house's bold forms
contain generous living spaces,
characterized by the architect's
interest in structural expression.

9

10

House at Alibag

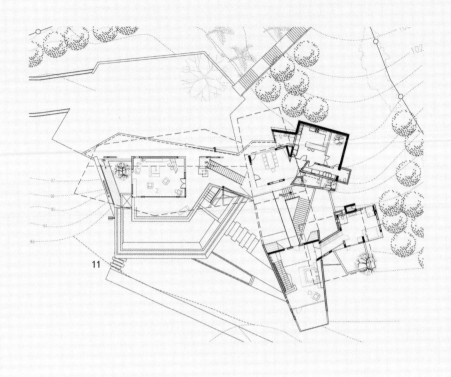

11, 12 Plans

New Settlements

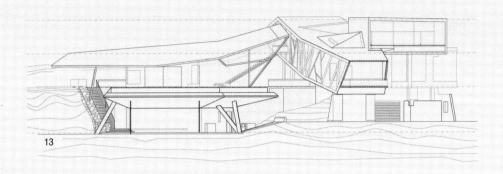

13

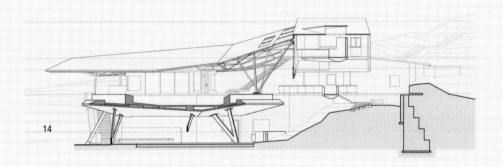

14

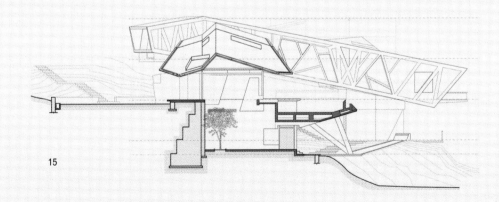

15

13, 14 Sections
15 Elevation

House at Alibag

Lagoon Residence
Alibag, Maharashtra
Malik Architecture

'The traditional detail of the Mangalore tiled roof, with its double-curved tiles and ventilation gaps, cannot be tampered with. The spacing of the tiles, battens and supporting members needed to be disciplined and rigid.'

Arjun Malik

Four years after completing the House at Alibag (p. 192), the opportunity to build another home presented the architect with a different set of constraints, in the form of a large number of existing trees. The site was densely populated with mature specimens, and there was no question of losing any with a diameter of 10 cm (4 in.) or more, so this house finds its place in between those trees where there was enough space for the required accommodation.

A well that had since dried up also informed how the house would be arranged, while a third organizational influence was the desire to create distance and distinction between communal and private spaces. The result was that the more formal entertaining spaces were positioned near the entrance, reserving areas set more deeply within the plot for family and close friends.

Responding to the client's admiration of Moorish architecture experienced on trips to Seville, architect Arjun Malik understood that water was integral to the house. Rather than working with the language of foreign architecture, however, he chose to develop the idea of the veranda as a key component of the design, with each associated with bodies of water that brought distinct qualities.

Malik looked closer to home for architectural references, drawing inspiration from the traditional Mangalore tiled roof, which incorporates double-curved ceramic tiles and ventilation gaps. This craft was employed in accordance with established traditions, with a team of skilled craftsmen from Kerala drafted in to complete this element of the construction. Innovation, however, was possible in the design of the supporting structure, which evolved into a language of repetitive asymmetric timber trusses, audaciously cantilevered from single footings.

The generous overhanging roofs vary in their geometry, with some reaching right down to the ground. Collectively, however, they establish a series of horizontal datum lines across the relatively flat site, bringing coherence and order to the planning of spaces that need to negotiate their position in among the trees. This horizontality is further emphasized by how the architect chose to integrate the revived well, which he excavated to create a hybrid of a hammam and a stepped well to form the focus of the principal entertainment spaces located close to house's main entrance.

1 As a development of the previous house, Lagoon Residence displays discrete elements of modern structural playfulness.

1

Lagoon Residence

2

2 While the gym was expressed as
a modern metal box, the dominant
architectural language draws on
traditional construction techniques.
3 The Mangalore tiled roof was the
architect's primary inspiration, either
bearing directly on the ground or,
as seen here, supported on large
branching columns.

New Settlements

4

New Settlements

5

4, 5 While timber is the predominant
material, accents of concrete and
glass are also used to create differing
degrees of enclosure.

Lagoon Residence

6

6 The bedrooms enjoy maximum privacy, sheltering beneath the same roof forms, but screened from the gardens by fine joinery panels.
7, 8 An existing well was revived and transformed into a sunken pool, recalling elements of the hammam and stepped well.

New Settlements

7

8

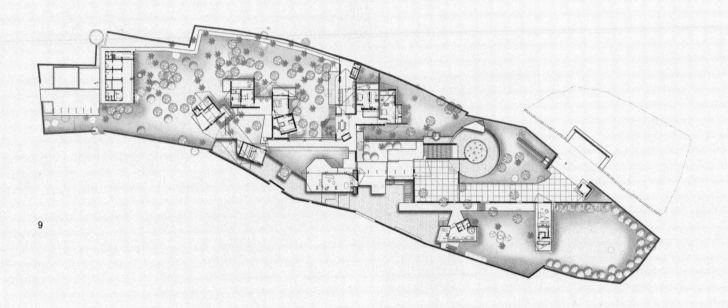

9

9 Plan

New Settlements

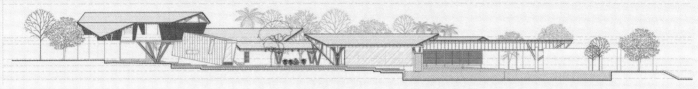

10

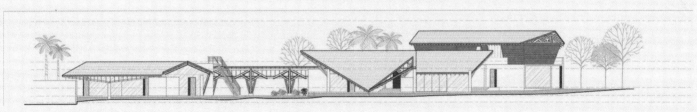

11

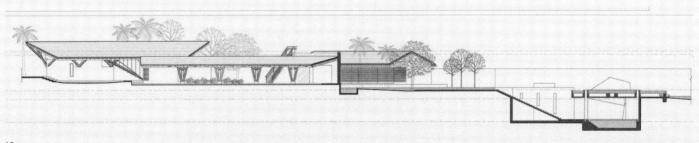

12

10, 11 Sections
12 Elevation

Lagoon Residence

House of Three Streams
Lonavala, Maharashtra
Malik Architecture

'We didn't want to interrupt the flow. We simply picked moments in which you could inhabit and build shelter, without breaking the movement of the landscape within the house.'

Arjun Malik

Located inland of Mumbai, where the climate is cooler and drier, is the third in this trilogy of Malik projects. Defined by its relationship to three large ravines that carry the monsoon flood, and to five historic forts that once occupied the area, it is described by its architect as influenced by memory and topography, with no need for abstract architectural ideas.

Formed on black basalt walls that emerge from the rocky water channels, the house is experienced as a series of terraced verandas that find their level and location between water courses and mature trees. Three primary roof forms coalesce through a series of geometric distortions to bring unity to a wide variety of spaces that, despite being largely single storey and ground-bearing, do, in fact, negotiate an 18 m (60 ft) fall across the site.

Clad in zinc, these generous timber structures open up and out onto an undulating landscape, which flattens out to address the lake and more distant panoramas beyond. They also bring shelter to the viewing platforms and a series of lightweight timber-and-glass pavilions, which are purposefully dispersed across the site to create distinct territories for each of the four generations that frequently come and live here together.

The memory of a historic fort wall tracks an edge between the two ravines and creates a dividing line across the site. This separates communal areas to the north and east from the more private bedrooms and dining spaces to the south and west, and marks a division that is further animated during the monsoon season, as violent torrents of water discharge from the hills above for four or five months of the year. Above this ravine, to the south of the site, sits an infinity pool that bridges the natural water course. Sitting above two children's bedrooms, the elevation of the pool is also a security measure, discouraging the attention of frogs, rats and snakes, who would otherwise seek out water sources during the region's prolonged dry season.

'We didn't want to tamper with nature,' explains architect Arjun Malik, 'but instead wanted to be absorbed into the flow of the site. Before building, we often came and sat here to synchronize ourselves with the rhythms of the seasons, the light and the contouring to see if any answers would emerge from the energy of the territory.'

1 This house responds to the landscape in an entirely different way to the approach used for the House at Alibag, using playfulness to evoke memories of the type of forts that originally occupied the site.

1

House of Three Streams

2

3

New Settlements

4

2–4 The fortified tower and wall
are used as organizing elements,
tracking the edge of two ravines.
Communal and private spaces are
placed on the land to each side,
unified by the oversailing roofs.

House of Three Streams

5

5–7 The oversailing roofs bring
shelter to discreetly screened living
rooms, open verandas and the main
circulation spaces in between.
8 (overleaf) At the end of one of
the accommodation wings, the roof
form is fully expressed, setting up a
dramatic relationship with the lawns
and verandas to each side.

New Settlements

6

7

House of Three Streams

House of Three Streams

9

10

New Settlements

11

9 An infinity pool not only sets up breathtaking relationships with the surrounding trees, but also provides some protection from frogs, rats and snakes.

10, 11 Private internal spaces are more conventionally accommodated in orthogonal buildings beneath the pool and terraces.

House of Three Streams

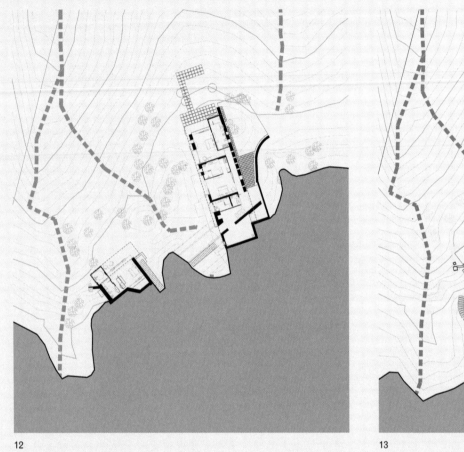
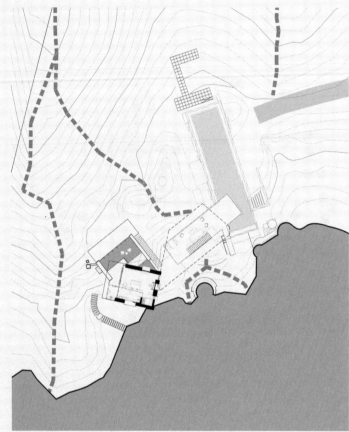

12

13

12–14 Plans

New Settlements

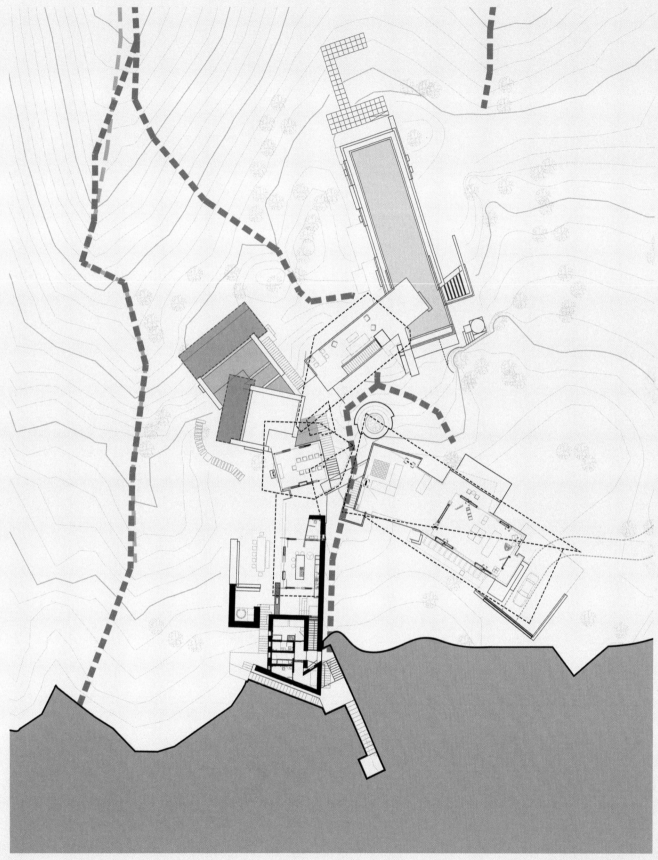

14

House of Three Streams

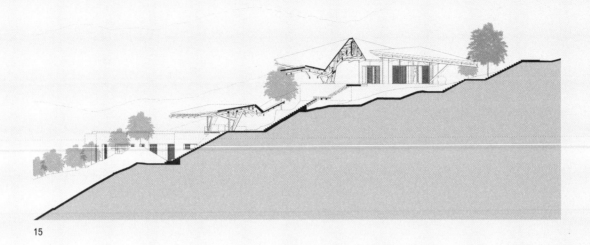

15

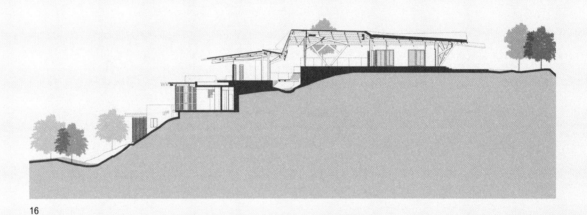

16

17

15–17 Sections

New Settlements

Four

Improvisation

Improvisation:
Serious approaches
to playfulness

Featured project

House of Balls
Ahmedabad, Gujarat
Matharoo Associates

As noted in the introduction to this book, one of the most tangible qualities of contemporary Indian architecture is how it exploits the notion of improvisation. Perhaps best summed up by the Hindi word *jugaad*, it is nearly always creative, with adaptations providing an innovative fix to make existing things work. It often relies on creating new things with meagre resources, and on occasion seeks solutions that bend the rules and rely on out-of-the-box thinking.

During my time at the *Architectural Review* (2003–12), one of the most prominent and prolific proponents of this sort of architecture was Gurjit Singh Matharoo of Matharoo Associates. Rising to fame with award-winning projects like the Ashwinikumar Crematorium and the Prathama Blood Centre (both 2000), his creativity continues today, with even greater playfulness and experimentation, and a level of can-do optimism and humour. This humour still persists, and was especially evident at the symposium I convened as part of the research for this book (see pp. 18–22), with Matharoo seizing the opportunity to critique the challenges and opportunities that go with working for some of the country's richest clients.

So as an endnote to this brief survey, serving as an antidote to what have been unapologetically presented as homes for India's super-rich, it seems fitting to introduce this final chapter on playful improvisation by revisiting one of Matharoo's most modest yet celebrated projects of all: the House of Balls, winner of the 2010 AR Emerging Architecture Award.

Cast in Matharoo's trademark rough concrete and animated by simple metal components, this bunker-like weekend house was designed for an aquarium shop-owner as a place of retreat and fish breeding – a curious blend of activity that has resulted in a place centred on four 9,000 litre (nearly 2,000 gallon) tanks forming a magical, cooling pool at the heart of the home. Occupying approximately 30 per cent of a modest plot of land, the house is arranged as a linear form along the length of the site's western boundary. Steeply contoured, the site allowed Matharoo

'Although clearly distinct from the houses that follow, House of Balls nonetheless has some things in common with them. All are in Ahmedabad, all are large houses and all are for a joint family set-up.'

Samira Rathod

1

2

1–3 On approach, the house presents a series of slim concrete fins that step out and overlap to screen the arrivals court from the garden and create a narrow point of entry.

3

House of Balls

4

5

4–7 From the garden, the composition is dominated by an array of fifteen concrete balls, which serve as counterweights to the metal screens enclosing the space within.

6

Improvisation

to partially bury the house, helping maintain the cool and stable environment the constant presence of water aids in establishing.

Entered from the south, the thin end of the concrete structure presents a narrow entrance leading directly into the principal space. Having passed a concealed cluster of rooms including a bedroom, kitchen and bathroom, to the left are the pools, with water visible through large vision panels that sit beneath a series of pressed-metal panels. To the right is a second array of panels above a long concrete counter to mirror the first.

Balanced by large concrete balls, each of the thirty panels are raised easily by hand, creating myriad combinations of light and shadow as the sun passes from right to left over the course of the day. In the evening, the sun sends playful and dynamic reflections into the main living space, which remains cool owing to the shade provided by a deep frame – an uber-brise soleil – which also functions as a garden seat, steps for children to climb on, and a bar and serving counter for entertaining guests, while also offering protection from the rain and repelling rats and snakes. Pink water lilies, multi-coloured tropical fish, a grassy knoll and the occasional roof-climbing cow complete the curious composition.

Fun and functional, this house typifies Matharoo's approach. It is also extremely frugal, with 125 mm (5 in.)-thick walls, beams and columns cast in steel shuttering with concrete that was mixed, poured and vibrated by hand. Everything is pared back to the minimum, to the extent that all services are hidden from sight, including a 50,000 litre (11,000 gallon) water tank (traditionally dug by hand), and a biogas plant that runs on cow manure. Even the concrete balls were handmade, cast inside cheap plastic balls, and simply suspended with almost invisible steel wire.

While this project, built for an incredibly low budget of £60/m² ($78/11 sq ft) in 2008, may be too agricultural and raw for many to consider living in, the projects that follow show how the architect has managed to use his persuasion and playfulness to apply an equally playful and dynamic creativity to the luxury-housing market – one that may otherwise remain slick, glitzy and way too cool for school.

7

8

9

10

8–10 When fully deployed, the
raised screens reveal a series
of unique interiors that include
an aquarium with four huge tanks,
where the owner's prized fish are
bred, and a cluster of enclosed
rooms for himself and his family.

Improvisation

1

Fissured Living

Fissured Living
Ahmedabad, Gujarat
Matharoo Associates

'The fissures are the nourishers and breathers for the home inside, breaking the structure to create lively entities, and making it difficult to say whether they split the blocks apart or hold them together.'

Gurjit Singh Matharoo

Like Moving Landscapes (p. 256), this house is also designed to provide independent living to a large, multi-generational family, made up of the families of two brothers and their aging parents. Unlike the former, however, this house uses masonry in a boldly static form to provide privacy, capture hidden treasures of the landscape and moderate the region's fiercely hot climate.

With almost no visible glazing, the house resembles, on approach, the ultimate built version of Minecraft – a series of monolithic stone forms piled up to create an imposing and fortified composition. The only concessions to that popular video game are the occasional circular column appearing inside and out, and the fact that the module is rectangular, rather than a pure cube. In deference to the house's name, the architect is keen to emphasize the space between the masses themselves, as small cracks on the exterior open up into large caverns within.

Recalling the organization of a vernacular settlement, in which clusters of accommodation come together to create a single place, here, distinct suites of rooms accommodate each family and the parents, as well as guests, and contain services. Each cluster is arranged around a large central living space the architect likens to a village square, or *chowk*, which becomes the centre of each family's social activity, articulated by a dramatic concrete stair that rises up two storeys, unifying and dividing the otherwise open space and allowing territories to be claimed by those who venture out of their own suites to share in this communal space.

At a more granular level, a similar degree of fragmentation is repeated in each of the main suites through the creation of niches and a variety of ceiling heights. This not only allows the large volumes to be broken down to a more intimate scale, but also blurs the boundary between inside and out, as the same spatial format is adopted in a number of external courtyards stepping in and out behind the privacy of the impenetrable walls.

Clad in economical local stone on the outside, the composition takes on the character and timeless quality of an ancient ruin, with blocks that have shifted over time and been reclaimed by nature as the plants within its crevices embrace the masonry.

1 (previous page) Even the staircase articulates the notion of narrow gaps as notional cracks in the solid rock.
2, 3 (overleaf) On approach, this home gives very little away, articulated as it is in the form of a pile of randomly stacked masonry blocks.

Improvisation

2

Fissured Living

3

Improvisation

Fissured Living

4

Improvisation

5

Fissured Living

6

Improvisation

7

6 In contrast to the solid exterior, visitors are greeted by a gravity-defying door that pivots on a centric axis to create a dramatic double-height entrance.
7 Interiors also exhibit a richer palette of materials, with concrete, steel, timber and fabrics set against elements of natural stone.

Fissured Living

8

8–10 At the heart of the home's cavernous communal space, this concrete stair acts as connector and divider, rising through three floors to create a dramatic filigreed screen.

Improvisation

9

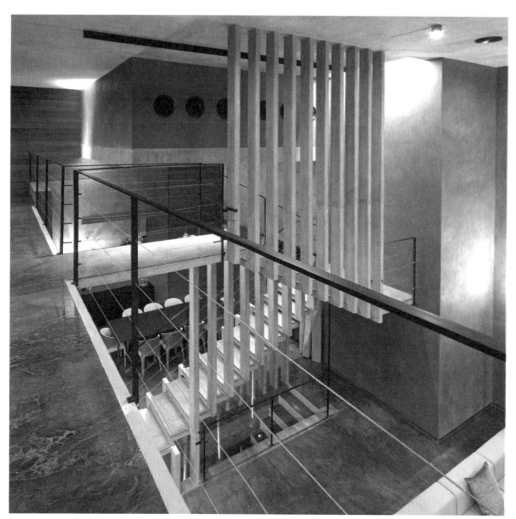

10

　　　　　　　　　　Fissured Living

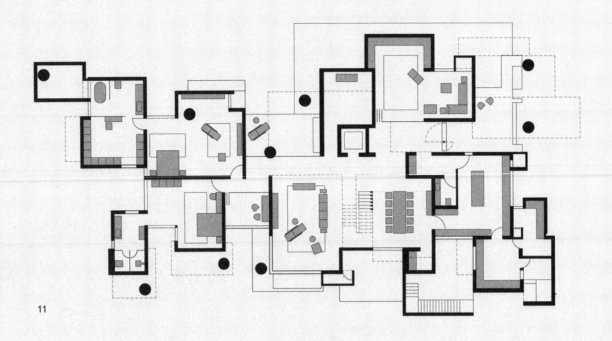

11

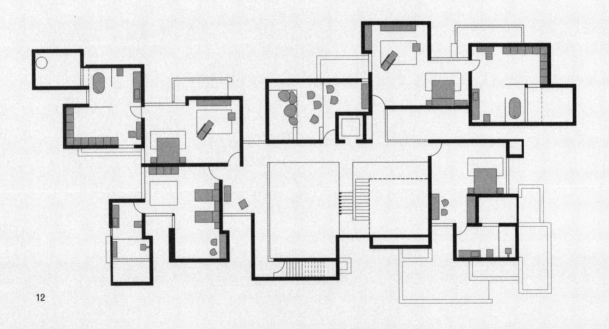

12

11, 12 Plans
13–16 Elevations

Improvisation

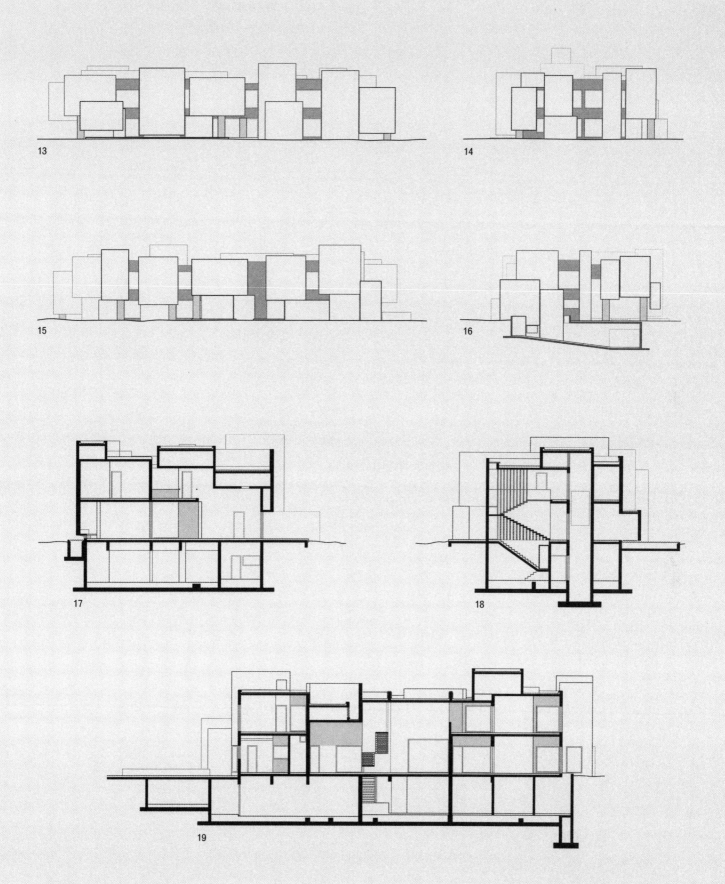

13

14

15

16

17

18

19

17–19 Sections

Fissured Living

Stripped Mobius
Ahmedabad, Gujarat
Matharoo Associates

'This seemingly infinite loop
of fluid planes in bare concrete
simulates a mobius strip, modulating
the space to be one that is inside
yet outside, contained yet open,
lofty yet intimate.'

Gurjit Singh Matharoo

This house, located on the outskirts of Ahmedabad and designed for a real-estate developer, extends and amplifies the themes explored in House of Balls (p. 226) and Fissured Living (p. 232) through its more overt combination of rectilinear and curvaceous forms and the design of its external walls, with both solid and porous elements.

Issues of privacy and communality were critical, as was following the principles of Vastu shastra, the ancient guidelines governing the shape and placement of spaces, water bodies and courtyards, down to the orientation of the loos and choice of colour. The name of the house refers to the presence of an apparently endless ribbon of concrete that threads its way through the otherwise rectilinear composition in plan and section, screening service areas, forming thresholds and enveloping the generous living space at the heart of the home, before rising up and around to form a gently undulating ceiling.

Externally, this element is subservient to and anchored by two double-storeyed rectangular blocks, which are expressed in darker Cuppadah sandstone and placed parallel to each other on the north–south axis of the site. To the east, facing visitors as they arrive, is the guest wing with formal areas including the entrance, living space, guest room and kitchen. Behind this, the wing to the west is more private, and contains the master bedroom, and bedrooms for the grandparents and both children.

Internally, the emphasis shifts away from the formality of the two main wings, as the void between them opens up to play host to family life. Here, the concrete form billows to give shape, character and dynamism to the main living and dining spaces, a temple and large verandas that open out to gardens. The house is deeply internalized and lit only by modest areas of glazing to the north and south, with a single ray of sunlight permitted from a single oculus in the centre of the concrete roof.

Further articulation celebrates the structural and visual fluidity of concrete, with continuous strips of light marking the roof junction between wings and mobius, teardrop-shaped openings and gently ramping stair guards, and, at its most extreme, in the fully expressed asymmetrical dome of the ground-floor prayer room, which brings a sense of topography to the open mezzanine. Beneath all of this sits the hidden entertainment room, another world entirely, where curved concrete forms persist, rendered with light from above and juxtaposed against simple glass screens.

1 This house exploits the versatility of cast concrete, shaped as it is with orthogonal and curvaceous forms. 2 (overleaf), 3 (pp. 248–9) The mobius form is articulated as a light concrete surface, threading its way around and through two blocks clad in Cuppadah sandstone.

Improvisation

1

Stripped Mobius

2

Improvisation

Stripped Mobius

3

Improvisation

Stripped Mobius

4

5

Improvisation

6

7

4, 5 The mobius envelops the
double-height living space,
articulated by a single oculus and
its corresponding ray of sunlight.
6, 7 Around and above the living
room, a naturalistic topography of
empty space serves as a generous
place of neutrality between the
communal space below and private
spaces beyond.

Stripped Mobius

8

9

8, 9 Around the perimeter of the
central space, smaller niches are
created, including a small temple.
10, 11 The whole house sits above
a generous basement, where
numerous recreational spaces
are hidden away.

Improvisation

10

11

Stripped Mobius

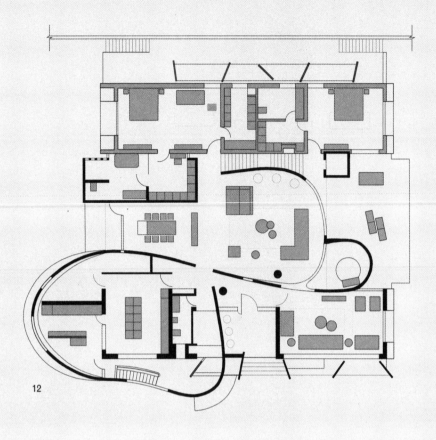

12

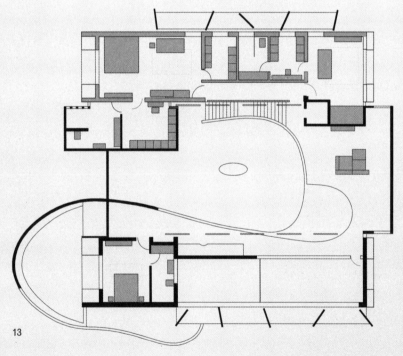

13

12 Ground-floor plan
13 First-floor plan
14 East elevation
15 South elevation

Improvisation

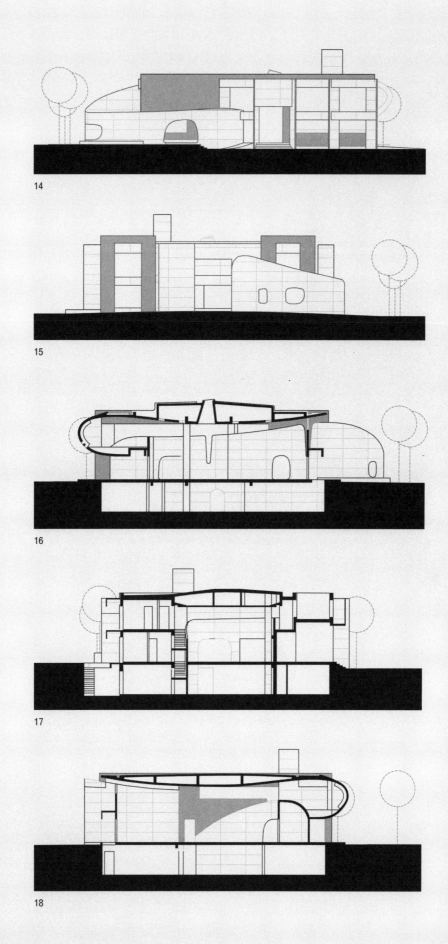

14

15

16

17

18

16–18 Sections

Stripped Mobius

Moving Landscapes
Ahmedabad, Gujarat
Matharoo Associates

'It is in the layering of space and screen that the house's entire envelope becomes an interface mediating between the artifice of the inside and verdant site outside.'

Gurjit Singh Matharoo

This house, also situated on the outskirts of Ahmedabad, was designed for one of the city's most prolific property developers, his wife, their two sons and several members of the extended family. Sitting within an enormous 20,000 m² (215,278 sq ft) plot, which the client shares with his two brothers, it comprises a three-wing pavilion, set against the margin of the site to create a courtyard at its heart. The side wings contain private spaces, including suites for each family, while the central range hosts the communal living space. Circular enclosures at the intersection of the wings contain utility spaces, stairs, a lift and a private external court.

It is against the backdrop of this static and well-balanced composition that architect Gurjit Singh Matharoo's dynamic play comes to life, as the apparently impregnable stone skin enclosing the entire perimeter of the house cracks open to reveal its obligatory glass heart.

At the push of a button, this imposing stone wall breaks down into an array of Bidasar stone panels – 5 m (15 ft) high, 3 m (9 ft) wide and 46 cm (1 ft 6 in.) thick – which spin gently about their centres or slide away to reveal the transparent cocooned interior. Matharoo explains that the idea came to him when he stumbled upon a piece of stone, and noticed how it contained a fossilized impression of an arid tropical landscape.

He immediately saw the possibility of this highly polished material in creating a moving landscape that would help blur the boundaries between inside and out, and set about designing the robust yet silky smooth mechanisms required to achieve the necessary tension between reality and illusion. While some slide and others rotate, the most audacious use of these massive panels is within the main courtyard, where double-stacks pivot independently, one atop the other, further exaggerating the system's dynamic gravity-defying effect.

There is a functional and performance-based justification for this spectacle, as the outer layer of stone panels help create a buffer between inside and out, protecting the glass and concrete interiors from the intense sunlight and 45°C (113°F) heat. As well as almost halving the projected energy load for air-conditioning, this space also doubles as passageway, veranda, entrance vestibule and circulation space, and provides essential protection from the monsoon. The use of stone extends further into elements of furniture and interior design, with lights that are machined out of alabaster, which, when illuminated, provides the most natural ambience.

1 The 'moving landscapes' are created through the ingenious mobilization of apparently massive panels of Bidasar stone.

Improvisation

1

Moving Landscapes

2

3

Improvisation

4

2–4 The house is articulated by a
range of screen types, with some
sliding or rotating on the ground
floor, and others pivoting, one on
top of the other, at higher level.

Moving Landscapes

5

6

Improvisation

7

5–7 Throughout the home, inside and out, the highly figured Bidasar stone is set against other key materials, including concrete, metal and glass.

Moving Landscapes

8

9

Improvisation

10

8–10 Beyond the dynamic external
stone walls, the interiors derive
distinction from spatial and material
diversity, with modern colourful
furniture adding a playful flourish.

Moving Landscapes

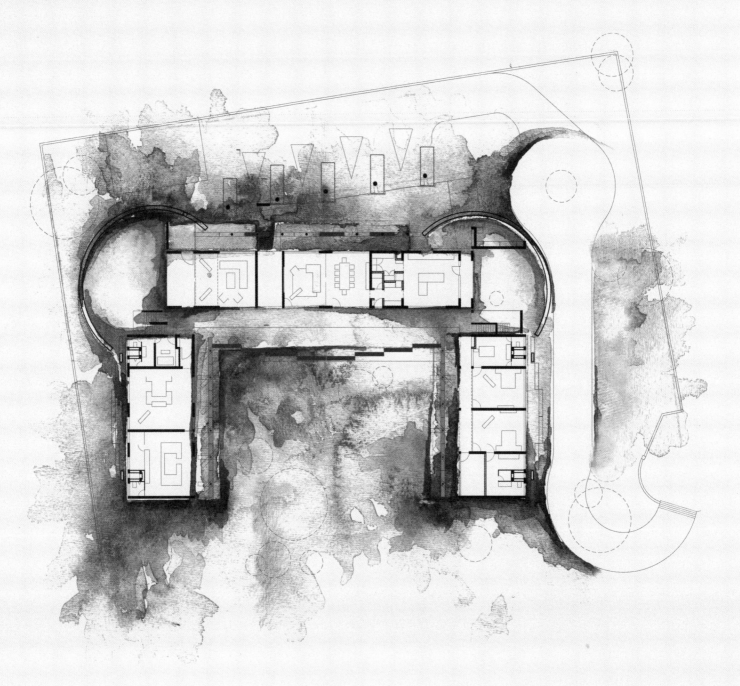

11

Improvisation

12

11 Floor plan.
12 Section.

Moving Landscapes

Architects' biographies

Abraham John Architects (p. 160)
Abraham John Architects is a multi-disciplinary firm founded in 1967, with Abraham John and Alan Abraham as joint principal architects. Projects include several charitable works, such as earthquake- and cyclone-proof buildings in Karaikal (Tamil Nadu), Vijayawada and Hyderabad (Andhra Pradesh), Latur (Maharashtra) and Rajkot (Gujarat). Alan Abraham served as professor at Sir JJ College of Architecture in Mumbai, and was recently named one of IGEN's top fifty architects and designers.

Architecture Brio (pp. 144, 172)
Mumbai-based Architecture Brio was founded in 2006 by Shefali Balwani and Robert Verrijt, who met in Sri Lanka and shared a mutual fascination with the work of architect Geoffrey Bawa (1919–2003). Balwani studied at CEPT University in Ahmedabad, later working with Rahul Mehrotra Architects in Mumbai and Channa Daswatte in Sri Lanka. Born in the Netherlands, Verrijt studied at the Delft Technical University, where his Master's thesis won the Dutch Archiprix award. He lectures extensively in India and abroad, and sits on the board of the Academy of Architecture, Mumbai.

Khosla Associates (p. 132)
Khosla Associates, based in Bangalore, was established by Sandeep Khosla in 1995, and is today headed by Khosla and Amaresh Anand. The practice has won over thirty awards, including WAN House of the Year 2017 for the Retreat in the Sahyadris, and the Bar/Restaurant Interior category at the Trends Excellence Awards 2018. In 2011, the firm was named by *Wallpaper* magazine as one of India's ten most innovative architectural practices, and by *Architectural Digest* as one of the most influential names in Indian architecture and design for six consecutive years (2014–19).

Romi Khosla Design Studios (pp. 46, 110)
Romi Khosla Design Studio is led by architect and artist Martand Khosla, who graduated from the Architectural Association in London in 2001, before returning to India and becoming a partner in the firm. Among his designs are the Castro Café (2010) and a hospice (2004) in New Delhi, which won the World Architecture Community award. Under Khosla's guidance, the firm has designed some of the most critically acclaimed buildings in India, including the LEED platinum-certified Volvo Eicher Headquarters in Guragon (Delhi), the first steel corporate building in the country. Khosla is currently designing the Indian Embassy in Uzbekistan, as well as interiors for Goldman Sachs and Greenply Industries, and a number of residential projects.

Malik Architecture (pp. 192, 202, 212)
Mumbai-based Malik Architecture is an award-winning multi-disciplinary design practice with over thirty-seven years of experience. Founder and principal architect Kamal Malik was born and raised in Shimla, in the Himalayas, and studied at the School of Planning and Architecture, New Delhi. Partner Arjun Malik received his B.Arch from the Rachana Sansad Academy of Architecture, Mumbai, returning to the practice in 2005, after receiving his M.Arch from Columbia University in New York. Ketan Chaudhary graduated from the L.S. Raheja School of Architecture, Mumbai, and joined the firm in 1992.

Matharoo Associates (pp. 226, 232, 244, 256)
Matharoo Associates was founded in Ahmedabad in 1992. The practice has won many awards, including the 2009 AR Emerging Architecture Award, the 2010 Architectural Review House Award and the 2011 Chicago Athenaeum International Architecture Award. Principal architect Gurjit Singh Matharoo studied at CEPT University in Ahmedabad, where he has been visiting faculty since 1990 and is currently Chair for Architectural Design. He is the founder member of the architectural workshop Pan India Travel Studio, and in 2013 was awarded an International Fellowship by the Royal Institute of British Architects, one of the youngest recipients of the honour.

Matra Architects (pp. 30, 38, 100)
Having moved to Germany when he was ten, Verendra Wakhloo returned to India twenty years later to set up Matra Architects, based in New Delhi. Among the firm's recent projects are the Gaurav Gupta shop in New Delhi and the Ranthambore Vatika Resort in Rajasthan. Wakhloo also worked at Vastushilpa Consultants, where he was influenced by the work of B.V. Doshi, and is a member of the Council of Architecture and the Indian Institute of Architects.

Sameep Padora & Associates (p. 68)
Sameep Padora is principal architect and founder of the Mumbai-based architecture studio. Having received his M.Arch from Harvard University's Graduate School of Design in 2005, in 2011 he was invited to speak at the Royal Institute of British Architects. In 2015 the practice's projects were the basis for the travelling exhibition *Projective Histories*, shown at the Somaiya Centre for Lifelong Learning, Mumbai. In 2016, Lattice House won *Wallpaper* magazine's House of the Year. Padora is a member of the Academic Council at the School of Environment and Architecture.

Samira Rathod Design Associates (pp. 154, 182)
Architect, furniture designer, writer and teacher Samira Rathod is principal of Samira Rathod Design Associates, founded in 2000 and based in Mumbai. She studied at the Sir JJ College of Architecture and the University of Illinois, Urbana-Champaign, and worked for Don Wald & Associates in California, before starting her own partnership in 1995. Rathod is an adjunct faculty member at the Kamla Raheja Vidyanidhi Institute for Architecture and Environmental Studies in Mumbai.

S&PS Architects (p. 56)
S&PS Architects was founded by Shilpa Gore-Shah and Pinkish Shah in 1997. They both studied at the Sir JJ College of Architecture and the University of New Mexico, Albuquerque, and have also lectured frequently in India and abroad. They have been visiting design faculty at the Kamla Raheja Vidyanidhi Institute for Architecture for over fifteen years.

Spasm Design (pp. 78, 120)
Spasm Design was founded in 1995 by Sanjeev Panjabi and Sangeeta Merchant, both graduates of the Academy of Architecture, Mumbai. The practice has thirteen staff members, and works on residential, commercial and mixed-use projects, both at home and as far afield as Tanzania. Having started off working on interior refurbishments and interventions, the firm now focuses on designing single-family homes, villas and office buildings.

Studio Mumbai (p. 94)
Architect Bijoy Jain received his M.Arch from Washington University, St Louis, and worked in Richard Meier's offices in Los Angeles and London (1989–95). After returning to India, he founded Studio Mumbai in 1995. His works have been presented at the Alvar Aalto Symposium, the Architectural League of New York and the Canadian Centre for Architecture, and he was a finalist at the Aga Khan Awards 2010. Jain is Norman R. Foster Visiting Professor of Architecture at Yale University.

Vastushilpa Consultants (p. 24)
Vastushilpa Consultants is a multi-disciplinary practice founded in 1955 by the Pritzker Prize-winner B.V. Doshi. Doshi worked for Louis Kahn, as well as Le Corbusier for four years as Senior Designer (1951–54) in Paris, followed by four more years in India supervising the master's projects in Ahmedabad. Doshi has been a member of the judging panels for the Indira Gandhi National Centre for Arts and the Aga Khan Award for Architecture. He is a Fellow of the Royal Institute of British Architects and the Indian Institute of Architects. Rajeev Kathpalia is a partner at the firm, and is the recipient of the Prime Minister's Award for Excellent in Urban Planning and Design and the 2019 Award for Distinction in Architecture from Washington University, St Louis. He has served as Honorary Professor at the Xia Jiaotong-Liverpool University, in Suzhou, China.

Project credits

Radhika Villa (p. 24)
Ahmedabad, Gujarat
Architects: Vastushilpa Consultants
Lead architect: Rajeev Kathpalia
Completed: 2009

Jenga House (p. 30)
New Delhi, Delhi
Architects: Matra Architects
Lead architect: Verendra Wakhloo
Project team: Priyank Jain, Shweta Jain, Hitesh Katiyar,
    Ankit Jain, Mukesh Kumar
Area: 1,675 m² (18,030 sq ft)
Completed: 2017

Kaleka Residence & Studios (p. 38)
Greater Noida, Uttar Pradesh
Architects: Matra Architects
Lead architect: Verendra Wakhloo
Project team: Rachit Shrivastava, Vinay Saxena, Mukesh
    Kumar
Completed: 2016

Brick House (p. 46)
New Delhi, Delhi
Architects: Romi Khosla Design Studios
Lead architect: Martand Khosla
Completed: 2017

Collage House (p. 56)
Navi Mumbai, Maharashtra
Architects: S&PS Architects
Lead architects: Shilpa Gore-Shah, Pinkish Shah
Liaison architects: Sopan Prabhu Architects
Structural engineers: Rajeev Shah & Associates
Electrical engineers: Praful Sonawane, Mahesh Sawant
Services consultants: Arkk Consultants
Site supervision: Amish Mistry Architect
Main civil contractors: Homework Constructions
Civil finishing works: Kantilal Suthar, Sawarmal, Jagdish,
    Jagrut Kumar
Fabrication: Deepak Mhatre, Shafibhai, Imam Steel, Furkan
    Sheikh

Aggregate plaster: Arvind Rathod
Glazing: Natwarlal Kawa
Plumbing: Ajay Majhi, Hussainbhai
Carpenter: Aditya Rana
Painting and polishing works: Bajrangi
Textured plasters: Junaid
Area: 520 m² (5,597 sq ft)
Completed: 2015

Lattice House (p. 68)
Jammu City, Jammu
Architects: Sameep Padora & Associates
Lead architect: Sameep Padora
Area: 465 m² (5,000 sq ft)
Completed: 2015

House of Secret Gardens (p. 78)
Ahmedabad, Gujarat
Architects: Spasm Design
Lead architects: Sanjeev Panjabi, Sangeeta Merchant
Project team: Ingit Anand, Kalpesh Shah, Mahendra Shah,
    Laxman Desai
Structural engineers: Ducon Consultants Pvt. Ltd
Landscape consultant: Kunal Maniar
MEP Consultant: Vimarsh Plumbing
RCC contractor: Mahir Builtcon
Interior civil contractor: Mortar
Manufacturers: B&B Italia, Baxter, Bespoke, Cocoon Fine
    Rugs, De Castelli, Delta Light, Durall Systems India,
    Flaminia, Fontana Arte, Giorgetti, Hansgrohe, Henge,
    iGuzzini, Jaipur Rug, JBR Coatings, Khazana, Kohler,
    Laufen, Lee Broom, Luceplan, Memo, Poliform, Poltrona
    Frau, Roche Bobois, Valdama, Panoramah!, Sidewalks of
    the World, Sources Unlimited
Carpenter: Krishna Interiors
Artists: Nabibakhsh Mansoori, Bhairavi Modi, Mansoor,
    Preksha Kapadia, Roma Patel
Completed: 2018

Belavali House (p. 94)
Kalyan-Dombivli, Maharashtra
Architects: Studio Mumbai
Lead architect: Bijoy Jain
Completed: 2008

Wood House (p. 99)
Satkhol, Uttarakhand
Architects: Matra Architects
Lead architect: Verendra Wakhloo
Site area: 12,142 m² (130,695 sq ft)
Area: 237 m² (2,551 sq ft)

Flying House (p. 110)
Dharamshala, Himachal Pradesh
Architects: Romi Khosla Design Studios
Lead architect: Martand Khosla
Area: 557 m² (6,000 sq ft)

House Cast in Liquid Stone (p. 120)
Khopoli, Maharashtra
Architects: Spasm Design
Lead architects: Sanjeev Panjabi, Sangeeta Merchant
Contractors: IMPEX Engineers
Engineers: Rajeev Shah & Associates
Area: 638 m² (6,867 sq ft)
Completed: 2013

Retreat in the Sahyadris (p. 132)
Maharashtra
Architects: Khosla Associates
Lead architect: Sandeep Khosla
Civil contractor: Canwill Constructions
Manufacturers: Accoya, Duravit, Grohe, Shree Sai Baba
    Marbles, Ritikaa Woods
Completed: 2017

Tala Treehouse Villa (p. 144)
Kuda, Maharashtra
Architects: Architecture Brio
Lead architects: Shefali Balwani, Robert Verrijt
Design team: Khushboo Asrani
Manufacturers: Hawa, Bharat Floorings
Soft furnishings: Nicobar, Pride, Shift
Client: Forest Hills, Tala
Area: 225 m² (2,422 sq ft)
Completed: 2017

Broacha House (p. 154)
Alibag, Maharashtra
Architects: Samira Rathod Design Associates
Lead architect: Samira Rathod
Completed: 2010

Villa in the Palms (p. 159)
Penha de França, Goa
Architects: Abraham John Architects
Structural consultant: BL Manjunath
Area: 610 m² (6,566 sq ft)
Completed: 2018

House on a Stream (p. 172)
Alibag, Maharashtra
Architects: Architecture Brio
Lead architects: Shefali Balwani, Robert Verrijt
Manufacturers: Acor
Area: 300 m² (3,229 sq ft)
Completed: 2013

Shadow House (p. 182)
Mumbai, Maharashtra
Architects: Samira Rathod Design Associates
Lead architect: Samira Rathod
Project team: Girish Bhadra, Rameshwar Bhadhwa,
    Jeevaram Suthar, Hasnain Kadiani, Ariff Abdulla
Structural consulant: Rajiv Shah & Associates
Area: 465 m² (5,000 sq ft)
Completed: 2017

House at Alibag (p. 192)
Alibag, Maharashtra
Architects: Malik Architecture
Lead architects: Arjun Malik, Kamal Malik, Ketan Chaudhary
Site area: 7 acres
Area: 1,068 m² (11,500 sq ft)
Completed: 2009

Project credits

Lagoon Residence (p. 202)
Alibag, Maharashtra
Architects: Malik Architecture
Lead architects: Arjun Malik, Kamal Malik, Ketan Chaudhary
Design team: Amit Modi, Sunil Gavane, Rucha Pimprikar
Structural engineers: Strudcom
Electrical engineers: Parth Electricals
Civil contractors, site supervision and glazing: Unique
    Construction Technologies
Landscape consultant: Design Consultants, Taera Chowna
Rainwater harvesting: Mungekar & Associates
Cladding: Vijaynath
HVAC: Cool Air Systems
Plumbing consultant: Suhas Gangan
Plumbing and firefighting: Khodiyar
Pools and water features: Silver Pools
Site area: 2 acres
Area: 2,079 m² (22,380 sq ft)
Completed: 2013

House of Three Streams (p. 212)
Lonvala, Maharashtra
Architects: Malik Architecture
Lead architects: Arjun Malik, Kamal Malik, Ketan Chaudhary
Area: 1,115 m² (12,000 sq ft)

House of Balls (p. 226)
Ahmedabad, Gujarat
Architects: Matharoo Associates
Lead architect: Gurjit Singh Matharoo
Project team: Hardik Pandit
Structural engineer: Rajendra Singh Matharoo
General contractor: Shriram Builders
Client: Mahesh Mohatta
Area: 130 m² (1,399 sq ft)
Site area: 530 m² (5,705 sq ft)
Completed: 2004

Fissured Living (p. 231)
Ahmedabad, Gujarat
Architects: Matharoo Associates
Lead architect: Gurjit Singh Matharoo
Completed: 2018

Stripped Mobius (p. 244)
Ahmedabad, Gujarat
Architects: Matharoo Associates
Lead architect: Gurjit Singh Matharoo

Moving Landscapes (p. 256)
Ahmedabad, Gujarat
Architects: Matharoo Associates
Lead architect: Gurjit Singh Matharoo
Project team: M.C. Gajjar, Avneesh Tiwari, Mohit Maru, Irene
    Giubinni, Shilpa Sushil
Manufacturers: Artemide, EDRA, MDF Italia, Casina, Flow
Structural engineers: Matharoo Engineers, Rajendra Singh
    Matharoo, Hitesh Rathi
Mechanical engineer: Harshad Jhaveri & Associates
Interior designer: Matharoo Associates
Landscape architect: Vagish Naganur
General contractor: Shree Ram Builders, Ahmedabad
Client: Trilok Goyal
Area: 1,900 m² (20,451 sq ft)
Site area: 3,500 m² (37,674 sq ft)
Completed: 2012

Directory

Abraham John Architects (p. 160)
31 Green Acre
Union Park Rd No. 5, Khar West
Mumbai, Maharashtra 400052
abrahamjohnarchitects.com

Architecture Brio (pp. 144, 172)
Vasant House, 19th Road, Khar West
Mumbai, Maharashtra 400052
architecturebrio.com

Khosla Associates (p. 132)
18 17th Main, HAL 2nd A Stage Indiranagar, Bangalore
560008
khoslaassociates.com

Romi Khosla Design Studios
(pp. 46, 110)
C-9, Maharani Bagh
New Delhi, Delhi 110065
rk-ds.com

Malik Architecture (pp. 192, 202, 212)
2nd floor, Kaiser-I-Hind
1/6 Currimbhoy Road, Ballard Estate
Mumbai, Maharashtra 400001
malikarchitecture.com

Matharoo Associates
(pp. 226, 232, 244, 256)
19, Pool, Pleasure Ville II, Nandoli Ahmedabad, Gujarat
382115
matharooassociates.com

Matra Architects (pp. 30, 38, 100)
53 Navjeevan Vihar, Malviya Nagar
New Delhi, Delhi 110017

Sameep Padora & Associates (p. 68)
Bungalow No. 22C
New Kantwadi Scheme, Bandra West
Mumbai, Maharashtra 400050
sp-arc.net

Samira Rathod Design Associates
(pp. 154, 182)
srda.co

S&PS Architects (p. 56)
1 Chandan, 8 BBCI Railway CHS
Vile Parle W
Mumbai, Maharashtra 400056

Spasm Design (pp. 78, 120)
310, Raheja Plaza
Shah Industrial Estate, Andheri (W)
Mumbai, Maharashtra 400053
spasmindia.com

Studio Mumbai (p. 94)
561/563 N.M. Joshi Marg Byculla West
Mumbai, Maharashtra 400011
studiomumbai.com

Vastushilpa Consultants (p. 24)
Sangath, Thaltej Road
Ahmedabad, Gujarat 380054
sangath.org

Acknowledgments

Eternal thanks to my beautiful wife Natasha, who let me venture to India when she was thirty-eight weeks pregnant. Fortunately, Zack Alexander didn't come early. This book is therefore dedicated to my family, 'G7': Natasha, Zack, Isla, Archie, Mia and Daniel. Thanks are also extended to all contributing architects and Surya Kakani, Dean of Faculty of Architecture at CEPT University, for making our specially convened Contemporary House symposium possible.
Rob Gregory

Working 5,000 miles away from home is never easy, and I would like to thank my family – Yuki, Cosmo and Lulu – for their understanding and forgiveness of my frequent absences; Sophia, Dennis and Susanne at VIEW Pictures for their enthusiasm and patience; Jonathan Bell at *Wallpaper*, who shared his interest in India and commissioned a series of shoots; architect Gianni Botsford, who recommended me for my first commission in India; and Sameep Padora, Gurjit Singh Matharoo, Virendra Wakhloo and Martand Khosla.
Edmund Sumner

First published in the United Kingdom in 2021 by Thames & Hudson Ltd, 181A High Holborn, London WC1V 7QX

First published in the United States of America in 2021 by Thames & Hudson Inc., 500 Fifth Avenue, New York, New York 10110

Contemporary House India © 2021 Thames & Hudson Ltd
Text © 2021 Rob Gregory
Photographs © 2021 Edmund Sumner

All plans and drawings supplied by the architects.

British Library Cataloguing-in-Publication Data
A catalogue record for this book is available from the British Library

Library of Congress Control Number 2020932059

ISBN 978-0-500-02133-0

Printed and bound in India by Replika Press Pvt. Ltd

Rob Gregory is senior campus architect at the University of Bristol and Lecturer at the University of Bath. He was previously senior editor of *Architectural Review* magazine and programme manager at The Architecture Centre. He has worked as a consultant critic and curator for RIBA, the Royal Academy and the British Council.

Edmund Sumner is a London-based architectural photographer, who has collaborated with leading architects from around the world since 1998. He has served as guest editor for both *Wallpaper* and *Architectural Review* magazines for their respective India issues, and focuses particularly on the work of emerging young architects in Japan, India and Mexico. Notable clients include Tadao Ando, RSHP and John McAslan + Partners.